# Transcending Capitalism through Cooperative Practices

# Transcending Capitalism through Cooperative Practices

Catherine P. Mulder

First published 2015 by
PALGRAVE MACMILLAN

The author has asserted her right to be identified as the author of this work
in accordance with the Copyright, Designs and Patents Act 1988.

Palgrave Macmillan in the UK is an imprint of Macmillan Publishers
Limited, registered in England, company number 785998, of Houndmills,
Basingstoke, Hampshire, RG21 6XS.

Palgrave Macmillan in the US is a division of Nature America, Inc., One
New York Plaza, Suite 4500, New York, NY 10004-1562.

Palgrave Macmillan is the global academic imprint of the above companies
and has companies and representatives throughout the world.

Hardback ISBN: 978-1-137-33987-4
Paperback ISBN: 978-1-349-57936-5
E-PUB ISBN: 978-1-137-33713-9
E-PDF ISBN: 978-1-137-33709-2
DOI: 10.1057/9781137337092

Distribution in the UK, Europe and the rest of the world is by Palgrave
Macmillan®, a division of Macmillan Publishers Limited, registered
in England, company number 785998, of Houndmills, Basingstoke,
Hampshire RG21 6XS.

Library of Congress Cataloging-in-Publication Data

Mulder, Catherine P.
    Transcending capitalism through cooperative practices / Catherine P.
Mulder.
        pages cm
    Includes bibliographical references and index.
    ISBN 978-1-137-33987-4 (hardback : alk. paper)    1. Social classes.
2.  Capitalism—Social aspects.    3.  Social action.    I. Title.
    HT608.M86 2015
    305.5—dc23
                                                                    2015015305

A catalogue record for the book is available from the British Library.

# Contents

# Acknowledgments

This research project stretched six locations and 36 months, and given the length of time it required and all the places I visited, my acknowledgments are many—I hope I don't forget anyone; if so, please know that it took more than a village and that I thank all who have been there for me with this project.

Firstly, this book would not be possible without the theoretical approach developed by my mentor and his dearest friend and colleague, Richard D. Wolff and the late Stephen Resnick. Rick and Steve both serve(d) as mentors, scholars, teachers, and friends to many; we have lost Steve but he will live forever through his contributions to our profession, his students, and through Rick. Their approach is now taking on a life of its own, and it's known as the "Amherst School of Thought" to many. Additionally, I would like to thank all the other members of the Association of Economics and Social Analysis (AESA) who amplify the richness of their lifelong endeavor.

I would like to thank Palgrave Macmillan for publishing this work, particularly Leila Campoli and Sarah Lawrence in their New York office. They have been generous and patient with me throughout this entire process.

There have been many family, friends, students, workers, and colleagues who have supported this endeavor, but some need special mentioning. Foremost, I want to thank my mother, Maureen Butler, whose ceaseless love and support, both psychologically and financially, have helped this book come to fruition. I also thank my father, who was my inspiration for this book, Henry R. Mulder, is a hardworking man who owns an eighty-year-plus-old family plumbing business that is now in its fourth generation.

His hard work and dedication made me look at the labor process in a way that had not crossed my mind in the past. It also made me look at how the "American Dream" of owning/running your own business can often be difficult and stressful, and that is why this book is dedicated to this honorable man.

My sisters Jeanne Mulder and Carol Mulder Kray, whose love gives me a sense of confidence, I thank you both immensely. I also thank Carol and her husband, Leo Kray, for giving me my two wonderful nephews. Their eldest son, Leo Kray Jr., who is now finishing his plumbing school education and continuing the family tradition, and his brother, Corporal Paul Henry Kray, USMC, who is currently serving our country—I am proud of you both.

Thank you to the two people that make my parents very happy—my father's wife, Judith Mulder, and my mother's husband, Dominick Caccamo. You made our families whole. I would be remiss in not mentioning how important my aunt Patricia Butler Corso is to my mother and our family. Aunt Patsy is mother to my cousin Mark, and grandmother to his wonderful kids Mark Jr., Stephen and his wife Jamie, and my goddaughter AnneMarie Lowrie, all of whom make me very proud. Moreover, though it has now been more than 11 years, we all still miss and think about my late grandmother who always had fun no matter what, Catherine Powell Butler.

My colleagues and friends in the economics department at John Jay College of Criminal Justice (CUNY), really gave me the big push to complete this book, particularly my former chair, Joan Hoffman, and my current chair, Jay Hamilton. But no less of a push came from Geert Dhondt, whose friendship for the last six years has been immeasurable. Thank you also to Ian Seda-Irizzary, Mathieu Dufour, Rita Taveras, and my new colleagues J.W. Mason, Joseph Rebello, and Michelle Holder, and particularly to my dear friend who we lost in the summer of 2014, Caroline McMahon—I think of you every day and I still cannot walk past your office without hesitating. It warms me, though, that you are now with your son Sean.

I thank Judy-Lynne Peters, Ned Benton, Chuck Nemeth, Patrick O'Hara, Marilyn Rubin, Adam Wandt, and Jessica

Gordon-Nembhard, my John Jay College colleagues who are always there for me. I also thank many of my students at John Jay College for reading and giving me their input on various chapters, particularly Urata Blakaj, Simone Smilie, and Claudia Reyes. In addition I thank my colleagues/friends and coeditors of the soon-to-be-published *Marxian Economics Handbook*, David Brennan, David Kristjanson-Gural, and Erik Olsen, who all showed patience when I missed a meeting or some other faux pas; we'll produce a great handbook together.

Susan Feiner and Bruce Roberts deserve my special gratitude since they were instrumental in so many ways in helping me develop ideas, share their Maine camp with me, but most of all for their friendship and humor. I also thank Elaine Bernard, the director of the Harvard Trade Union Program and another mentor of mine. Elaine is a woman who is truly dedicated to her students, workers, and justice.

Another special thank-you to Evelyn Gort-Friedman for always making sure I had lunch and/or dinner during the crunch time as I finished this book. She and her husband, Steve Friedman, are truly good friends and neighbors. Whenever I needed something from the store or whatever, Evelyn was happy to help! Also to my dear friend Marylou Amarosa who was always there to listen, go out for a meal, offer unquestioning support, and—best of all—be my companion at numerous Broadway shows for those "downtimes."

A special shout-out of thanks to Shellie Gallagher, whose phone calls from Indiana always kept me laughing and/or feeling very special. Additionally, though so far away, Reshela DuPuis always had my back. Moreover, if it weren't for Brenda Shelley-McIntyre, this book would still be in my head and certainly not on paper.

Thank you to some colleagues and friends from other institutions who were kind enough to read, write letters of support for my work, and be a constant source of support: Antonio Callari, Richard MacIntyre, George DeMartino, Drucilla Barker, Suzanne Bergeron, and David Ruccio. And to Serap Kayatekin and Marcus Green, editors of *Rethinking Marxism*, for all their kindness and support.

Because I visited every site written about in this book, I have some extra thanks to my hosts. By chapter:

2. The London Symphony Orchestra: A special thank-you to archivist Libby Rice who filled in many blanks and became my friend while I was in London. I also thank all the LSO headquarters staff and any of the musicians I met. I also want to mention that, while in London, I went to quite a few LSO symphonies and other events—it made my research enjoyable.

3. The Lusty Lady: I visited San Francisco at a very stressful time—indeed it was the beginning of the end of this first unionized cooperative in the sex industry. While these are pseudonyms, I do thank Fred for her input on the union, and Princess Pandora and Delinqua for helping me understand the Lusty in a very unexpected way.

4. The New Era Window Cooperative: When I asked Armando Robles why he was so willing to speak openly with me, he said quite frankly that he wanted his grandchildren to read about what he had done and to be proud of him. I didn't ask Ricky Maclin the same question, but he let me know in no uncertain terms that he too was taking these risks because of his 6 children and 16 grandchildren. Thus, I dedicate this chapter to the Robles and Maclin grandchildren. Thank you, Armando and Ricky and all your colleagues at New Era who took the time to speak with me, at UE, and The Working World, particularly Brendan Martin.

5. Organopónico Vivero Alamar: I thank all of the workers and our hosts who were present during our visit to this unique urban farm in Havana, Cuba, which truly exemplifies how cooperation is not only possible, but also successful. Our group received such a wonderful education about organic farming and the post-Soviet era changes.

6. The Green Bay Packers: When I began thinking about including the Packers as a case study, I thought that it would be difficult to gain access to their organization. Happily, I was wrong—given the welcome by their public relations director Aaron Popkey and his colleague Sarah Quick—no one could have asked for better hosts. They invited me onto the field for the annual shareholders' meeting, gave me tours, and set up a

meeting with CEO Mark Murphy, who was more than amenable. In addition, I want to particularly thank one of the board members, Ms. Susan Finco, who helped me further understand the affection Green Bay has with its Packers.

7. Syracuse Cooperative Federal Credit Union: I would like to acknowledge one of my favorite people and dear friend Sharon Moran. Sharon is an associate professor at SUNY College of Environmental Science in Syracuse, NY. Sharon, at the time, was a member of the Syracuse Cooperative Federal Credit Union's board of directors and was instrumental in giving me access not only to the treasurer and to the operation, but also to one of their fundraising events where I met and spoke to donors, board members, and loan/grant recipients. I truly thank Ron Ehrenreich for all the time and information he provided me.

Last but certainly not least, this book would not at all be in the form it is in if it were not for the tireless editorial assistance of Judith Chien. Judith and I have been working together for many years, but there is no better editor. She is extremely patient, understanding, and really one of the sweetest people I have ever met. Her professionalism and efficiency are second to none.

Parts of this book were financially supported by the John Jay College of Criminal Justice's Economics Department's travel funds, as well as a PSC-CUNY Type B grant and the CUNY Faculty Fellowship Program. I thank all my colleagues in the latter for their input and support, particularly Thomas Volscho.

# CHAPTER 1

# Transcending Capitalism through Cooperative Practices

## Introduction

> When numerous workers work together side by side in accordance with a plan, whether in the same process, or in different but connected processes, this form of labour is called co-operation . . . Not only do we have here an increase in the productive power of the individual, by means of co-operation, but the creation of a new productive power, which is intrinsically a *collective* one. (Marx, 1976, 443; emphasis added)
>
> [. . .]
>
> When the worker co-operates in a planned way with others, he strips off the fetters of his individuality, and develops the capabilities of his species. (Ibid., 447)

When Marx made the above comments in his first volume of *Capital*, he was referring to a capitalist class process and commodity production that often requires workers to act collectively. While he abhorred the capitalist mode of production, Marx clearly did espouse another, more equitable work organization, one built on cooperation and devoid of the *chains* that bind workers—whether imposed by a capitalist or by a central government. Capitalist production can and does exist in centrally planned "Communist"[1] economies (Mulder, 2015). This type of production is NOT what Marx envisioned as *the* answer to capitalist exploitation. He stated:

> In its simple shape, as investigated so far, co-operation is a necessary concomitant of all production on a large scale, but it does *not*

in itself represent a fixed form characteristic of a particular epoch in the development of the capitalist mode of production. (Ibid., 453; emphasis added)

Marx simply demonstrated how workers can and do cooperate even under the harshest conditions. Even slaves and serfs in their respective modes of production cooperate with each other. The fundamental issue at hand is that it does not matter whether or not the cooperation is voluntary.

For over a century and a half now, the terms *Communism* and *Marxism* have conveyed such a profound negativity to many, that discussing the evils of capitalist production is not even within the mainstream economics discourse. Indeed, most college economics programs, both undergraduate and graduate, dismiss such discussions entirely, opting instead for the neoliberal neoclassical economics that many students find either too mathematical and abstract or completely unrealistic. Even the most conservative business students think the level of theoretical abstraction in their economics courses is far removed from actual business practice, while the more radical left students look to other disciplines that do not historically include capitalism's apologists. Scholars, activists, presidents, champions of industry, and the couple down the block may hold particular political, social, and economic opinions, but rarely does one hear or speak of any alternatives to the capitalist system. Instead, there is talk about more or less government control, involvement, and resources, and these debates resemble an old-fashioned metronome, never going far to one side or the other and then resting in the middle. In the United States, for example, members of both major parties, some of whom are themselves capitalists, are but minions and are dependent on the capitalist system for financial support, no matter how great their personal wealth may be. The campaign finance debates have brought this issue to light, but, given the 2010 decision by the US Supreme Court in *Citizens United v. Federal Election Commission*, which essentially gives corporations *carte blanche* in campaign financing, a major overhaul seems highly unlikely. As we will see, there are alternatives to the capitalist system, and they need to be celebrated, discussed, and supported—socially, culturally, and economically.

The alternative offered here is one of worker cooperation and production, without essentializing ownership or control, or in other words, a Worker Self-Directed Enterprise (WSDE) organizational structure (Wolff, 2012). It is apparent to me that Marx believed workers could arrange themselves into a collective enterprise without capitalist or some other exploitative type of supervision, thus giving me a venue and theoretical space in which to advocate for true worker justice, not simply for the typical liberal agenda of getting more crumbs from capitalists as trade unionists and other activists have been attempting to do since the dawn of capitalism (Mulder, 2009). It is obvious that workers have the knowledge, the skills, and the ability to work collectively. Of course, capitalist workers are paid wages; however, as will be developed more fully below, workers do not receive the full value of the goods and/or services they produce. This extra value goes directly to capitalists; in other words, *exploitation* exists. Cooperative alternatives to capitalist production exist, have existed, and are increasingly becoming much-preferred modes of production, as the obvious contradictions and failures of many capitalist enterprises become apparent. As Marx states:

> Cooperative factories provide the proof that the capitalist has become just as superfluous as a functionary in production as he himself, from his superior vantage-point, finds the large landlord. (Ibid., 511)

I believe that while most of his voluminous work is devoted to a critique of capitalism, Marx saw collective enterprises as a viable system of production. This can be seen particularly in his scholarly works, but also in his more "popular" speeches and writings for the "masses." An illustration of the latter can be found in his *Inaugural Address*, delivered to the International Workingmen's Association in 1864:

> But there was in store a still greater victory of the political economy of labor over the political economy of property. We speak of the *co-operative movement*, especially the co-operative factories raised by the unassisted efforts of a few bold "hands." The value of these great social experiments cannot be over-rated. By deed instead of by argument, they have shown that

production on a large scale, and in accord with the behests of modern science, may be carried on without the existence of a class of masters employing a class of hands; that to bear fruit, the means of labor need not be monopolized as a means of dominion over, and of extortion against, the laboring man himself; and that, like slave labor, like serf labor, hired labor is but a transitory and inferior form, destined to disappear before associated labor plying its toil with a willing hand, a ready mind, and a joyous heart. In England, the seeds of the co-operative system were sown by Robert Owen; the workingmen's experiments tried on the Continent were, in fact, the practical upshot of the theories, not invented, but loudly proclaimed, in 1848. (Marx, 2000)[2]

While most Marxian scholars agree that Marx abhorred capitalism, it is surprising that throughout history, he has been seen as a champion of centralized, government-controlled economic systems rather than as an advocate for cooperative enterprises without the fetters imposed by a tyrant, whether a Communist dictator or a capitalist.[3]

The existence of multiple cooperative enterprises—from the large-scale Mondragon system to small collective farms—is evidence that there is an alternative way to organize production processes. Admittedly, not all such enterprises are successful, and there are a variety of reasons for this, including legal, economic, social, and cultural factors. It is nonetheless clear to me that workers can organize themselves in a manner that is more flexible, and family and environmentally friendly. Most importantly, workers can make decisions about production and the distribution of the fruits of their labor, while working in an environment that is neither alienating nor dehumanizing. This book presents an investigation and a Marxian economic analysis of six case studies of productive cooperation in different forms. It provides the reader not only with the tools with which to develop such an enterprise, but also underscores some of the economic, political, and cultural processes that can either encourage or undermine cooperative endeavors to transcend capitalism. However, this discussion differs from others in that I do not assume that an enterprise constitutes an alternative to capitalism simply because it is a cooperative; it may or may not be, it depends on how work is organized and structured. Cooperatives, no matter how well intentioned, may be of any class structure, including capitalist. Therefore, careful review and investigation are imperative if one is to understand the various class processes or non-class processes that define the organization of a particular worksite.

### Capitalism in Crisis: It Is Time for Alternatives

The recent global economic crisis—or crises—in both industrial and non-industrial nations has prompted vociferous debates. But rarely is there evidence of discussion within the mainstream about the transformation of the dominant capitalist economic system into a more functional and equitable one. Since 2008, we have witnessed rampant unemployment and underemployment, firms closing or going overseas in search of higher profits, a level of environmental degradation that is unprecedented, banks and other financial institutions decreasing credit availability while simultaneously taking unnecessary risks and receiving government bailouts, increasing income and wealth inequality, with US corporate profits more than doubling in the years 2003 to 2011.[4] The typical hierarchical capitalist enterprise structure and the institutions that support it are obviously failing to provide good jobs that come with some economic security, and this affects not only the employees' families but also the communities in which they live. Moreover, national, state, and local governments are watching their tax bases dwindle, and they have reacted by implementing harsh austerity programs that intensify instability and nervousness among the affected citizens. In this uncertain and obviously unsustainable situation, alternatives to capitalist economic structures should be assessed to discern their viability in such a turbulent global economy. Cooperative practices might be implemented by communities, organizations, and/or by the workers themselves, resulting in an enterprise arrangement that is more equitable, rational, democratic, and sustainable than the prevalent capitalist model. Institutions such as trade unions and credit unions could also have vital roles in transcending capitalism.

This book analyzes six diverse workplaces that are examples of democratic and cooperative alternatives to the conventionally accepted capitalist model. The cases include the London Symphony Orchestra, the Lusty Lady, New Era Window Cooperative, the Green Bay Packers, and the Syracuse Cooperative Federal Credit Union. These enterprises show that alternatives to capitalism are attainable and often preferable to and possibly more sustainable than their capitalist counterparts, even under cultural, political, and economic conditions that do not support them.

Each case is examined using the methodology of New Marxian Class Analysis (NMCA). Although it was I who coined the term NMCA (Mulder, 2009), the concept itself was developed by Stephen Resnick and Richard Wolff in their seminal work, *Knowledge and Class* (1987). This methodology allows the researcher to clearly delineate the agent(s) responsible for workplace decisions, in order to evaluate whether said workplace is democratic, cooperative, capitalist, or follows some other mode of production. When using NMCA, the primary question addressed is this: who makes the production and surplus distribution decisions in the enterprise? "Laborers are understood to do a certain amount of labor sufficient to produce the goods and services their current standard of living requires. Marx called this 'necessary labor.' However, laborers in all societies perform more than necessary labor. They do what Marx calls 'surplus labor'" (Resnick and Wolff, 1987, 20). If the answer is that decisions are made collectively by the workers, then economic democracy has been achieved. A democratic workplace is one in which the workers make all the decisions about the production, appropriation, and distribution of any revenues they produce. That is, each worker, or his/her elected representative, gets one vote on all workplace issues. New Marxian Class Analysis (NMCA) methodology to present, assess, and discuss the various cases that demonstrate the successful achievement either of workplace democracy or of community participation via ownership and/or membership in a cooperative enterprise. If, on the other hand, the workers do not self-appropriate the surplus they created, then some other kind of economic structure is in place, typically the capitalist class structure that predominates in today's society. Indeed, as has been shown elsewhere, capitalist class structures may exist in both non-profit and for-profit institutions, and may be in both the private and public sectors (Mulder, 2015). This refutes the neoliberal and radical left arguments that maximizing profits and private ownership alone define a capitalist enterprise (Mulder, 2015; Resnick and Wolff, 2002). Economic or workplace democracy is empowering because it provides stability for the workers and their communities and often leads to the choice of environmentally friendly production methods—after all, the workers live in the communities where the enterprise is located. And finally, if workers make the decisions, inequality and worker exploitation can be lessened or even completely eliminated.

The primary objective here is to demonstrate that it is not only possible for economic alternatives to capitalism to exist, but that they also may have longevity and can even thrive under the laws, norms, power, and access to financing that capitalists typically enjoy. However, severe struggles are often involved. In fact, in the case of the Lusty Lady, the struggles were dire and after many years of turmoil, the business closed on Labor Day, 2013.[5] Each case study illustrates how democratic practices function within the particular institution under discussion. While "economic democracy" will be sought in each case, it is already clear that two of the six cases are *not* examples of economic democracy. They are nonetheless examples of sustainable alternatives to the traditional for-profit capitalist model. The Syracuse Cooperative Federal Credit Union, for example, is a membership cooperative, which supports other firms' pursuit of economic democracy by making credit available to them and providing other financial and administrative support, including writing business plans, investments, and providing other information to help these firms survive and perhaps even flourish. The second is the case of the Green Bay Packers, which many have erroneously deemed an example of community ownership. However, a closer analysis reveals that the Packers are not owned solely by members of the community of Green Bay, Wisconsin, but by thousands of shareholders in all fifty states and in many other nations. As we will see, Green Bay Packers shareholders earn no dividends from the shares they own, nor can they sell their shares on the open market. Shares hold essentially no cash value (ESPN, 2012). The only right shareholders receive is to attend the annual shareholders' meeting. The Packers are nevertheless a truly remarkable case study. Not only are the Packers vital to the Green Bay economy; if the organization were to be sold, all the proceeds of that sale would revert to the Packers Foundation charitable enterprise in Green Bay.

## What Is New Marxian Class Analysis (NMCA)?

First developed by Richard Wolff and Stephen Resnick, the methodology of class analytics is utilized in this book. However, I believe the term New Marxian Class Analysis is more apropos than simply "class analytics." In an email communication with me, Professor Wolff explained that he and Professor Resnick did not adopt the term, fearing that it was too "provocative or immodest" and that the word "new" might imply that some other methodology is "out-of-date" or "old." But, he said, "for others to use it seems fine with me, and frankly I like seeing it used that way so long as you make clear what exactly this "new" theory is."[6] NMCA is an *antiessentialist* Marxian methodological approach used to analyze a particular site of production, whether private, public, for-profit, or non-profit. Whereas many Marxist scholarly activities focus on or use as their "entry points" issues of ownership and/or control of the means of production, "an antiessentialist or nonreductionist theory refuses to look for the *sine qua non* of any event because it does not presume that it exists. An antiessentialist theory understands every theory (including itself) to be inherently partial, a particularly focused intervention in social discourse" (Resnick and Wolff, 1987, 2). While ownership and/or control may reinforce or provide conditions of existence for capitalist firms, focusing primarily on these factors often veils the underlying class dynamics that may impede progress to a more just and democratic arrangement.

As one would expect, "New Marxian Class Analysis" indicates a methodology derived from the writings of Karl Marx, particularly from his more scholarly work such as the three volumes of *Capital* and *Theories of Surplus Value*. His popular speeches and writings were typically addressed to the masses, and he often "simplified" his analysis so as to better explain it. This is not to say that Marx was condescending to the workers he addressed; on the contrary, he was their fierce defender and advocate. However, he evidently did what many scholars do when addressing a diverse audience, putting his thoughts into a more accessible prose. Marx deplored capitalism, particularly the way it alienated workers from the fruits of their labor, and so, rather than extolling capitalism's virtues as many of his contemporaries and predecessors did, he uncovered its vileness. Marx did *not* develop a systematic alternative economic structure that included dictators and central government planning, as many have claimed for well over a century. Indeed, these types of schemes were generally equivalent to private capitalist institutions, except that they were implemented by the state rather than by individuals (Mulder, 2015; Resnick and Wolff, 2002). Marx did, however, methodically critique capitalism, giving the best explanation to date of its inner workings.

While NMCA may not be "new" to Marxists, it is "new" to Marxian scholars who have traditionally focused their research on the entry point of either power or ownership. Marx emphasized the *class* relationships and processes and unveiled the legal "social theft" that capitalists perpetrated on their employees. Simply put, he emphasized that workers produced more than what was necessary for their own subsistence and were forced, typically unbeknownst to them, to relinquish any excess (surplus) to the capitalists. This fact was often undetected, or possibly deliberately omitted, from the analyses of Marx's predecessors and contemporaries, and the same is true today. Even the quintessential "father of economics," Adam Smith, attributed to workers the value added to all commodities. Indeed, Smith contended that the source of the "Wealth of Nations" was the workers' productive capacity (1991). Nonetheless, Smith neglected, whether consciously or not, to highlight the work process within capitalism, and instead of being critical of it, he praised its contributions to economic growth and social advancement.

Like Marx, the NMCA framework focuses on the production, appropriation, and distribution of surplus value. Specifically, one can discern the particular operative mode of production, or the economic structure, simply by identifying who produces the surplus and who appropriates it. If the surplus appropriators are not the same as its producers, then the particular mode of production is exploitative. While NMCA is quite straightforward, its great value lies in its ability to uncover exploitative economic structures wherever commodities are produced, whether or not for a market. For example, NMCA has been applied to the household (Fraad, Resnick, and Wolff, 1994), to jails (Bair, 2007), to education (Aoki, 1994), to baseball (Weiner, 2003), to trade unions (Annunziato, 1990), and to musicians (Mulder, 2009; Seda-Irizarry, 2013).[7]

Although Marx discussed five discrete modes of production: ancient (primitive), slave, feudal,[8] capitalist, and communist, and although he supported *cooperative* enterprises, it was his critique of capitalism that was most prominent in his work. Given the vast inequalities and crises for which global capitalism is responsible, many have sought alternatives, such as cooperatives or collective enterprises, or a WSDE mode of production. It is vital to note that cooperatives, whether producer-, consumer-, or worker-structured, are not limited to a single mode of production. Indeed, worker cooperatives could be capitalist within the NMCA framework. The six case studies presented here offer such alternatives or support them. In the current cultural, political, natural, and economic climate in which enterprises exist, deviating from the generally accepted capitalist model is often discouraged. Often, this hegemony causes those seeking alternatives to be shunned, making it virtually impossible for their businesses to thrive, or even to survive. This was the unfortunate case with the Lusty Lady, as we will see in Chapter 3.

### Why NMCA?

NMCA's efficacy enables researchers to reveal the intricacies of enterprise structures and relationships and to discern their place within or outside capitalism. In a capitalist enterprise, for example, the capitalists, in the form of a board of directors, are the first and direct appropriators of any surplus value. Within the antiessentialist NMCA framework, issues of ownership and power over the means of production do not define the particular mode of production in question; however, ownership and power may provide critical conditions of existence for a capitalist enterprise's self-preservation or its reproduction. For example, although the members of the board of directors may not "own" the company or even a single share of the enterprise, they do appropriate the surplus value produced by the workers, which gives them the auspicious title of capitalist.

What makes NMCA different from more traditional Marxian class analyses is that the word *class* is an adjective that describes a particular process, for example a slave class process. It describes a process under which workers toil, and furthermore, it reveals who reaps the rewards from their efforts: "Class is understood as a distinct social process. . . . It is the economic process of performing and appropriating surplus labor" (Resnick and Wolff, 1987, 26). Surplus labor is the amount of necessary labor that workers perform "to produce the consumables customarily required by the direct producer to keep working" (ibid., 115). Unlike capitalism, in which workers earn wages for their necessary labor and receive no payments for the surplus labor they produce, a WSDE is a democratic and collective enterprise, one in which the workers directly appropriate and distribute the surplus. Of course, some of the distributions may be statutory, such as taxes, rents, and interest payments, as is also the case for capitalist firms. Nonetheless, in at least four of the six cases discussed here, it is for the most part the surplus-producing workers who make these distributions, mandatory or not.

Surplus labor is produced in every mode of production, but the particular class process under examination becomes evident only when the appropriator of the surplus has been identified. In a capitalist class structure, the capitalists, not the workers who produced the surplus, immediately appropriate the surplus value produced by the workers. Conversely, in a WSDE class structure, the workers who produce the surplus are in fact its collective appropriators. Moreover, as I have expanded elsewhere, when someone other than its direct producer appropriates the surplus, the workers are *exploited* (Mulder, 2009). Surplus that is "appropriated directly and immediately by nonlaborers . . . is Marx's precise definition of exploitation" (Resnick and Wolff, 1987, 20). The goal of Marxian scholars should be to rid workplace exploitation and the various processes that secure its conditions of existence, such as private property rights, lending requirements, "rugged individualism," and the myriad constraints put on alternatives to capitalism. This goal may sound lofty or even utopian, but as will be seen in the pages to come, noncapitalist enterprises do exist—admittedly, with their challenges—and they have endured.

One would generally think that self-appropriation or collective appropriation of the fruits of one's labor is preferable to someone else's seizing it; thus, one would think that a WSDE or collective class process would be preferred to that of a capitalist class process. Instead of using the word "communism" in this book, I choose to use the term WSDE because of negative connotations the word evokes, even though it is qualitatively and quantitatively different from the "Communism" practiced in the USSR and elsewhere. The USSR Communism advocated "central planning," where someone other than the workers decided what to do with the surplus they produced. The democratic economic process to which I refer adopts the notion that the surplus-producing workers should appropriate and subsequently distribute any surplus they produce. Thus, they are identified as Worker Self-Directed Enterprises.[9] Among the researchers who use the NMCA methodology, there is a debate about surplus labor "self appropriation" and whether or not it is self-exploitative. Often, the "American Dream" is to be a sole proprietor; however, such firms have a very high failure rate, and often the owner/worker is isolated and "works him/herself to death." This book focuses on collective/WSDE appropriation, and I will not enter the self-exploitation debate here (Hotch, 1994). Why would workers not want to earn the full amount for what they produced? Why is it that workers gladly hand over any surplus to their bosses? The answers are too complex to explore here, but culturally, politically, and economically, at least in the industrial world, most people come to realize that they will inevitably work for someone else. In the US educational system, for example, children are indoctrinated from a very young age about the marvels of capitalism. As I have written elsewhere, even trade unions rarely question the relationship between capital and labor; they see it as adversarial, but more often than not, they do not seek change as will become quite evident in the pages to follow (Mulder, 2009). Indeed, Marx also thought this was a limitation of the labor movement when he stated:

> Trades Unions work well as centres of resistance against the encroachments of capital. They fail partially from an injudicious use of their power. They fail generally from limiting themselves to a guerrilla war against the effects of the existing system, instead of simultaneously trying to change it, instead of using their organised forces as a lever for the final emancipation of the working class, that is to say, the ultimate abolition of the wages system. (Marx 1997, *Value*, 62)

Thus, the legal theft by capitalists of any surplus produced by the workers, however morally and ethically reprehensible it may be because of its exploitative nature, is the accepted norm not only for the "thieves" but also for the "victims" and their representatives. The number of challenges to this norm is increasing, however, and the six cases addressed here will highlight the possibility of alternatives. It should be noted, however, that although the chosen six cases are diverse and interesting, the groups contained therein may not have transformed themselves or come into existence to challenge capitalism. They may not even realize that they do indeed constitute an alternative to capitalism.

## NMCA Explained

While it may seem to be prioritized, *class* is merely the entry point chosen by NMCA to precisely expose sites of exploitation—whether they are found within a workplace or elsewhere. The word *class* is a modifier of a particular process that elucidates and underscores the production, appropriation, distribution, and receipt of the surplus created. A *class* process is an economic process unlike other economic, cultural, natural, or political processes that do not have a direct relationship to the surplus and are therefore referred to as non-class processes. By focusing on *class* processes, we are able to isolate the difference between those workers who produce surplus (productive workers) and those who do not (non-productive workers). The distinction between workers is important because it facilitates a thorough understanding of the unique and particular social construction in which these workers toil—which may, for example, give rise to understanding why some workers choose not to join particular unions (Mulder, 2011).

To begin our NMCA, we first look at commodity production and ask, who is producing them? Commodities, within the Marxian context, may be either goods or services, produced either for self-consumption or for someone else; they are produced for either or both market and non-market consumption; and they can be produced in either or both the private and public sectors of any society/economy. Commodity production however, does not happen in a vacuum, as many economists (and other social scientists) would like us to assume. For example, in just about every introductory economics textbook, the first chapter commences with an explanation about how "economics" is done—with models and the use of the *ceteris paribus* assumption, that is, "holding all else constant" while a specific topic, concept, issue, variable, or whatever is analyzed. We lose many potential economics students at this juncture because of the absurdity of this unrealistic assumption or entry point. To be fair, the assumption is later "relaxed" so as to "shock" the model in an attempt to explain a particular point; for example, if income were to increase, then the demand for "normal goods" would increase, and *voilà*, the commodity's price would increase for each and every level of quantity demanded. The expectation that "relaxation" will occur, however, can hardly be considered realistic. On the other hand, the NMCA methodology rejects the *ceteris paribus* assumption, which is but one of the many aspects that differentiates it from the other methodologies. New Marxian analysts view all processes, including commodity production and consumption, as *overdetermined* with an infinite array of both endogenous and exogenous variables that influence and are influenced by each other.

The ontological and epistemological theoretical position of overdetermination was "borrowed" by Resnick and Wolff "from

Freud, Lukács, and Althusser"; however, they admit that that they "considerably modified" it (1987, 2). They explain it in this way:

> To say that theory is an overdetermined process in society is to say that its existence, including all its properties or qualities, is determined by each and every other process constituting that society. Theory is the complex effect produced by the interaction of all those other processes. . . . The process of theory exists as the site of a particular interaction of all the influences stemming from all the other processes comprising any society. *In this sense these other processes are all the conditions of existence of the process of theory.* (Ibid., emphasis added)

NMCA thus rejects *all* essentialized/deterministic social theories, economic or otherwise, because they are reductionist, whether produced by mainstream or heterodox economists (ibid., 49). Essentialist economists look to specific variables and choose one (the *endogenous* variable) that is a function of some *exogenous* variables that can cause (influence) it to fluctuate. Thus, predictions are made and economic policies ensue. The recent and prolonged economic crises may provide some evidence that these models are at the very least problematic, and, more often than not, detrimental to workers' livelihoods. Within the NMCA framework, no *exogenous* variables exist. Therefore, the use of *ceteris paribus* is rejected because it negates, or at least obscures, the reality and/or the totality of the subject at hand. For example, an infinite array of economic, cultural, political, and natural processes overdetermine commodity production and consumption.

NMCA divides production into two distinctive class processes, the fundamental and the subsumed, to facilitate understanding the specific site under investigation. In the fundamental class process, surplus labor is produced and appropriated, while in the subsumed class process, the surplus is distributed and received. The same person could occupy various class positions within either the fundamental or subsumed class process; that person may also occupy non-class positions within the same job title or enterprise. For example, within capitalism, workers occupy the fundamental class position of surplus-value producers, while the capitalist holds the fundamental class position as appropriator.

That same capitalist also holds the subsumed class position as the surplus distributor, and any *direct* payment recipients of the surplus also holds a subsumed class position. Moreover, surplus-producing workers (productive workers) may also hold a subsumed class position as recipients of some of the surplus they produced, as is the case with many unionized workers who earn more than their non-union counterparts. This is known as the "union wage effect," a term first developed by Harvard economist John T. Dunlop in 1942. Basically, it is a wage premium union members enjoy while non-unionized workers do not. In NMCA this extra wage is considered a subsumed class payment. To further clarify, most capitalists are not the direct sellers of the commodities they produce; they sell them to retail outlets such as Walmart or car dealerships (Mulder, 2011). The capitalists sell their commodities to vendors at a discount otherwise know as the "wholesale" price. Thus, the commodity-producing capitalists make a subsumed class payment in the form of a discount directly to the vendors, and the vendors hold a subsumed class position of surplus recipient.

Subsequently, in order to resell the products, retailers often hire their own workers to secure their conditions of existence as subsumed class as surplus recipients. Those employees, while vital to the realization of the surplus value, are not *direct* surplus recipients, and thus are considered to hold non-class positions. This does not imply, however, that the retail workers are not valued or important in capitalist reproduction. On the contrary, they facilitate and ensure that the circuit of capital is completed. However, there is a distinct difference in the NMCA framework between the original workers who produce the commodity and the retail employees who sell it. The former are said to be "productive" workers because they *produce* surplus value, while the latter are considered "non-productive" workers because they add no additional value to the commodity in question (Mulder, 2011).

NMCA makes the distinction between productive and non-productive workers, and so their roles and responsibilities are unambiguous. The distinction is also important in the discussion of "exploitation." Surplus-value producing workers are exploited, while those who produce no surplus value are not exploited, no matter how they are treated by their employers. In a previous article, I showed that Walmart retail workers, who are indeed maltreated, abused, underpaid, and overworked (to name only a few atrocities the world's largest retailer commits), are not *exploited* in the Marxian sense. New and different suggestions about improving working conditions are needed; many have been tried but unfortunately failed. However, since the writing of this chapter, Walmart has announced that it will raise the minimum wage it pays its workers to $9 per hour.[10] The distinction between productive and non-productive workers should not and does not make a value statement regarding which worker is more critical to capitalist production, but it is an important distinction nevertheless. Furthermore, the delineation between the different class processes and the position of their occupants can either foster alliances or highlight contradictions that may prove to be critical in assessing avenues for improvement.

## Benefits of NMCA

Besides the obvious benefit of understanding and possibly rectifying worker exploitation, NMCA gives researchers leeway to delve deeper into the issues and problems faced by the workers in a particular enterprise or industry and also discerns how communities and their representatives might react/vote/plan. Unlike capitalists, for example, workers typically live relatively close to their workplaces, and if they participated in decisions regarding their working conditions, they might also consider local community economic development and more sustainable (environmentally friendly) technologies. Enterprise goals and management would differ significantly from those of typical capitalist corporations. For example, the same workers who make surplus distributions to secure their conditions of existence as WSDE workers would also want to make their living environments and their communities more worker- and family- friendly.

Another benefit of using the NMCA approach is that it gives workers and communities a different theoretical perspective and could result in prices lower than those charged by a capitalist firm for the same product; worker contentment might trump profit maximization. If the focus is not solely on profit maximization, but rather includes community development, worker democracy, and sustainable living conditions, the product's price, particularly in the case of monopoly pricing, might diminish. Currently, however, many worker cooperatives are "boutique" enterprises, with prices that are often higher than those of their competitors, thus making their longevity questionable. Overcoming that reputation will not be easy. Moreover, today's worker cooperatives tend to be small businesses with few workers, and so they cannot achieve economies of scale or the power over their suppliers to demand that the cost of necessary inputs be reduced. There are, however, some large-scale cooperative enterprises, which will be discussed in more detail below. We will consider specifically the case of Mondragon in Spain (and elsewhere) and its relationship with the United Steelworkers, and the Evergreen Movement in Ohio. There are also organizations that are making truly concerted efforts to promote cooperative workplaces; however, they often fall short of the economic democracy defined in this book using New Marxian Class Analysis.

One could speculate on a number of other benefits that could be derived from NMCA, such as showing how poverty could be reduced, workplace discrimination abolished, workplace injuries decreased, and such worker fringe benefits as pensions, maternity/paternity leaves, health care, flexible schedules, and child care increased. The limitations of NMCA are defined only by the limits of one's own imagination. One critical problem that would be immediately rectified if the workers collectively appropriated and distributed the surplus would be the ever-increasing gap between the chief executive officer's salary and that of the average worker. NMCA shows us that when the surplus labor is appropriated collectively and the board is elected by the workers, rather than by wealthy non-employee stockholders, the board's charge can be radically different from simply maximizing profits. If the surplus-producing worker-members charged the board with maximizing profits, it would have to abide by the group's decision. There is nothing in the NMCA framework that ensures cooperation and other more ideal conditions; however, it does allow us to envision a workplace different from the one that currently exists.

Nonetheless, this new worker-elected board is subservient to the members. The workers may or may not vote to pay the board members for their service and additional responsibilities. Within the NMCA framework, this payment would be a subsumed class payment, a distribution of the surplus to the board for these extra assignments. In such a case, the board members would hold the subsumed class position of surplus recipients. Workers could also receive additional subsumed class payments for attending meetings or any other responsibilities they might assume. In such a case these workers would hold various class positions: first, they would occupy a fundamental class position as surplus producer; second, they would also occupy the fundamental class position as surplus appropriator; third, they would distribute the surplus, thus occupying a subsumed class position; and, finally, the board members would receive a subsumed class payment, and thus hold the subsumed class position as surplus recipient.

In some instances, the surplus-producing workers may decide to hire managers, specialists, and a support staff to facilitate the enterprise's commodity production, as in the case of the London Symphony Orchestra (LSO). Chapter 2 includes a discussion of how the LSO members hire both managers and staff to do various tasks that free up the musicians to focus on producing music and on other responsibilities they might have. These workers, both the managers and the staff, because they are *directly* employed by the surplus-producing musicians but do not themselves produce music (in other words, produce no surplus), hold subsumed class positions as surplus recipients. In this particular case, these subsumed class participants do not participate in the political process of governance, but that does not negate the critical contributions they make toward the surplus realization and the success of the orchestra.

A very different organizational structure was in place at the Lusty Lady: *all* of the workers, surplus-producing or not, could participate in the political process of governance. Moreover, *all* of the workers were allowed to decide whether or not to join the collective and participate in any of its governance. That is, they were not required to become members of the cooperative, but most chose to do so. Thus, within the NMCA framework, some non-surplus-producing workers (unproductive workers) occupied a fundamental class position as surplus appropriators, and a new set of struggles could and (as we will see) did ensue. While it might seem desirable to have every worker, whether productive or not, participate democratically within the workplace—determining the types of work, the amount of work, possibly even the variety in skills and/or education—it can add to workplace tensions and therefore compromise the very existence of the enterprise. It is, however, possible for the productive workers to collectively appropriate the surplus while instituting a democratic practice to decide how to share it, the size of it, or other such matters.

The delineation of the particular class and non-class positions that workers occupy is central in the NMCA methodology, for it enables researchers to recognize whether or not exploitation exists and if so, how it might be eradicated. Moreover, establishing the various positions workers hold also allows us to understand the complicated and often intricate and sometimes even contradictory associations workers contend with daily. Researchers can illuminate or isolate the positions, depending on the focus of their study. For example, if the agenda is to uncover places where workers could form alliances with workers in other industries or firms, their class or non-class positions would show the commonality with other workers or could be used to better understand their differences.

## Cooperatives Vis-À-Vis Worker Self-Directed Enterprises

In his most recent book, *Democracy at Work: A Cure for Capitalism*, Richard Wolff has opted to use the term Worker Self-Directed Enterprises (WSDE) instead of the volatile "communist enterprise." In an email exchange with Professor Wolff, I asked him to tell me why he chose to do this, although of course I am acutely aware of the resistance in the popular press to the word "communist." Professor Wolff's response was:

> Since the goal was to focus above all on the analytics—how and why Marx's surplus analysis leads to the notion of changing the capitalist system at the micro level of the enterprise by means of productive

laborers appropriating the surpluses they produce—it seemed a major distraction to call such enterprises "communist." That word had been loaded with a set of associations—definitions that would have required laboriously stripping them away in order to get readers/listeners to the analytical core of the argument. It seemed faster, easier, and the wisest course to introduce the argument by means of a new term, admittedly awkward but logically connected to the argument: WSDE. (Wolff, December 23, 2013)

Given his reasoning and how "loaded" the word "communism" is, WSDE is chosen for analysis here.

According to the Independent Welding Distributors Cooperative (IWDC), a group for independent cooperatives, there are five main types of cooperatives: worker, consumer, producer, purchasing, and hybrid.[11] There are currently approximately 30,000 cooperatives and about 350 million participants in the United States, this number may be inflated given that there is a large number of people who belong to many cooperatives (Nadeau, 2013, 7). Although these estimates vary, it is safe to say that cooperatives in one form or another have a significant impact on the US economy. Cooperatives differ in size and scope, but typically have a quite commendable moral business ethos. Indeed, the International Cooperative Alliance (ICA) defines a cooperative as "an autonomous association of persons united voluntarily to meet their common economic, social, and cultural needs and aspirations through a jointly-owned and democratically-controlled enterprise" (ICA, 2015).[12] Furthermore, the ICA and other cooperative associations adhere to seven principles: "Voluntary and Open Membership," "Democratic Member Control," "Member Economic Participation," "Autonomy and Independence," "Education, Training, and Information," "Co-operation among Co-operatives," and "Concern for Community" (ibid.).

Most of the literature on worker cooperatives and economic democracy, while admirable and well intentioned, essentializes the ownership of the means of production and the democratic principle of one worker, one vote (Alperovitz, 2011; Dahl, 1986; Ellerman, 1990; Nadeau, 2013). Other researchers espouse community ownership/control and environmental sustainability

(Engler, 2010) and make suggestions about how to develop a cooperative enterprise. These studies are very helpful, and each identifies potential problems and offers strategies to overcome them. Class processes, as in the production, appropriation, distribution, and receipt of the surplus are often ignored, however. Thus, the analyses fall short of advocating a true WSDE, one that is arranged in such a way that the surplus-producing workers are identical to the distributors. WSDE members might form alliances with other cooperatives and their sympathizers to promote new legislation that supports alternatives to capitalism.

## Case Studies

Each of the six case studies presented here will be discussed using the NMCA methodology to demonstrate whether or not *true* economic democracy exists within each enterprise, in other words whether it is a WSDE or whether some other mode of production is in operation. Furthermore, even if the firm's class structure is not a WSDE, it may have a role in either supporting these firms or supporting its community and its members. In four of the six cases, the workers have union representation, and so there will be particular emphasis on how this representation aided or hindered cooperative practices.

The London Symphony Orchestra (LSO) is the first case study presented. As will be demonstrated, the LSO is indeed a democratic, worker-run institution, and basically a WSDE that has withstood the test of time even though it exists in a hegemonic global capitalist environment. To be completely a WSDE, an enterprise must be one in which the surplus- producing workers make *all* surplus production and distribution decisions. The LSO to some extent exemplifies this. It has been self-governing for over a hundred years, and indeed, the musicians who produce the surplus by performing live music—this is the commodity in question—are its *direct* appropriators. Two caveats will be elaborated on within the chapter though.

The second case study is the Lusty Lady peep show that was located in San Francisco, California. The "Lusty" was the first worker-run, cooperative, unionized firm in the sex industry in the United States. In 1996, the workers, who had become frustrated with often discriminatory, arbitrary, and capricious edicts imposed on them by the owners, organized themselves into a collective and joined the Service Employees International Union (SEIU). In 1997, the Lusty Lady was the only club of its type to be unionized. Eventually, though, because of competition from newer alternatives in the sex industry, such as Internet pornography, the Lusty owners faced decreasing profits and decided to sell the club. The workers, determined not to lose their jobs and livelihoods, purchased the club collectively in 2003. It was impossible for them to find traditional means of financing—after all, the only collateral the workers had was their labor power, which traditional US banks do not recognize as a commodity.[13] The cooperative members had no alternative other than to negotiate with the prior owners to hold the note; after reaching this agreement, the workers paid it off expeditiously. But although the workers were now the owners, they chose to remained unionized, which introduced new tensions and contradictions, particularly during the collective-bargaining process and when grievances arose. During my January 2013 research trip to San Francisco to interview the Lusty workers and union representatives, these tensions became quite evident. A comprehensive NMCA in Chapter 3 will include a discussion of these tensions and contradictions. It is ironic that many tensions occurred because the workers were unionized. Unfortunately, due to an exorbitant rent increase imposed by the landlord, who happened to be "associated" with the Lusty's major competition, Déjà Vu, the Lusty Lady closed its doors on Labor Day weekend, 2013. Meanwhile, Déjà Vu has reportedly taken control of all of the sex clubs in San Francisco and is the largest enterprise of its kind in the world.[14] The Lusty's conditions of existence were compromised due to a variety of political (legal), cultural, and economic processes that surrounded them. A thorough NMCA presented in Chapter 3 will uncover the various class and non-class processes that may have contributed to the Lusty Lady's demise.

In Chapter 4, the NMCA framework is used to investigate the case of New Era Window Cooperative in Chicago, Illinois. When beginning the research for this book, my plan was to show how the United Electrical, Radio and Machine Workers of America (UE) missed an ideal opportunity to help transform this company from a capitalist enterprise to a WSDE. In 2008, the owners of Republic Windows and Glass (the former name of the firm) declared bankruptcy and announced the imminent closure of the factory. Furthermore, Bank of America cancelled Republic's credit line, which eliminated severance pay and payments for unused sick leave and vacation time. The workers subsequently staged a sit-down strike, which resulted in their receiving those payments. The UE responded by successfully seeking a new owner/capitalist in Serious Materials. Serious hired back only a fraction of the workers and in early 2012, it announced that the factory would close, whereupon the workers staged yet another sit-down strike.

The primary issue here is that the UE did not originally facilitate the workers' takeover of the company and instead upheld the status quo, with the result that Serious remained a hierarchical capitalist workplace. The UE is known to be a progressive union, and its overlooking the opportunity to transform this workplace into a collective, democratic enterprise in 2008 is inexplicable. Finally, in 2012, when the workers received notice that Serious was closing, the workers, with the assistance of UE, Local 1110, purchased the company and are now running it themselves under the name New Era. The restructured firm is much smaller than Serious, but at my meeting with the workers during a summer 2013 research trip, they clearly demonstrated just how dedicated, even adamant, they are about maintaining a WSDE and democratic structure. Unlike the Lusty Lady, whose union, the SEIU Local 790, did not facilitate the revolutionary change in one mode of production to another. Instead, it was the workers who made these changes for themselves. New Era is also a unionized cooperative, but their class structure, in the NMCA framework, is a textbook example of a WSDE class process. Moreover, the union's role was and continues to be a significant facilitator in the hoped-for success of this small but remarkable firm.

Chapter 5 is an analysis of a Cuban Organic Urban Garden (Farm), Alamar Organopónico UBPC. This is an example that with state support (not simply financial) a transformation from state capitalism to worker (economic) democracy (a WSDE) is not only possible, but also more efficient, cheaper, and more sustainable than its traditional counterparts that use chemicals in their fertilizer and experience much waste. This enterprise model, which is becoming increasingly popular in Cuba, is one example of an organic urban farm. Since 1992, Cuba has sought alternatives to state-run enterprises due to the collapse of "Communism." In the NMCA framework, in a traditional state-run enterprise, workers do not make production and distribution decisions; thus, the enterprise structure exemplifies "state capitalism." Now, however, Cuba is promoting and supporting worker-run collectives like Alamar, which embrace economic democracy. I visited this farm in June 2012, and I found that it is truly is a fertile site for further discussion and analysis.

The next case addressed is that of the Green Bay Packers football organization. The Packers are a professional US football team located in Wisconsin that has been in existence since 1923. While many believe that it is a community-owned institution because the mainstream press proclaims it to be so, it is not owned by Green Bay—indeed, its "owners" are from all fifty states and from a variety of countries. This case deviates from the previous ones in that it is an example of how a single enterprise can help a community avoid the devastation that has been befallen many small cities and even some large ones. Indeed, if not for the structure and bylaws of the Packers organization, scarcely anyone would know of Green Bay, Wisconsin. Although the Packers are *not* an example of a WSDE workplace or economic democracy for its productive workers, the football players, this enterprise has kept Green Bay and Brown County from the economic and social ills that have plagued many similar communities. There are two very interesting aspects of the Packers organization that will be further explored using the NMCA framework. One of these is the fact that this non-profit enterprise is constrained by its own bylaws to remain in Green Bay; if the team were sold, it could not be moved to another city, and all of the proceeds of the sale would go directly to the Green Bay Packers Foundation, a charitable organization. Also of interest is the role of the owners of the Packers, who receive only "bragging rights" of ownership and the right to go to the annual shareholder meeting at the Packers' Lambeau

Stadium, which is more like a "tailgate party" than a meeting. Many of these owners, unlike those of every other NFL team, are working-class people and union members themselves. During the 2012 NFL lockout, the contradictions faced by these owners came to the forefront, making the Packer organization a truly interesting and rich site of production to investigate and include in this book.

In the concluding chapter, I investigate an institution that is dedicated to financing cooperatives and other alternatives to typical capitalist firms. A community/consumer cooperative, the Syracuse Cooperative Federal Credit Union (SCFCU) is a member-run institution that strives to give primacy to the local economic development of Syracuse, New York. Founded by progressive activists in the 1980s, SCFCU is owned and managed by its members. Like other financial institutions, it holds deposits, provides checking accounts, and makes loans to individuals and businesses. Unlike the customers of traditional banks, however, all SCFCU depositors are members and have equal voting rights—that is, one person, one vote. Loans are also atypical in that SCFCU provides them to local individuals and enterprises that have been rejected by more traditional banks because they are deemed "risky" or are nonconventional. The loans are generally made to local cooperatives that employ "green" technologies or engage in "fair trade" as opposed to "free trade." Home mortgage loans are also made to local Syracuse residents who might not be funded by a for-profit bank for many reasons.

In the final chapter, I suggest avenues for other enterprises that might transform into democratically run businesses and also delve into the various institutions, laws, culture, and other obstacles that may be impeding such transformations. I synthesize the case studies and offer strategic suggestions for class transformation—also known as a revolution when there is a change in the mode of production. A comparison of the enterprises highlights pitfalls and shows how they can be avoided or overcome. Additionally, I address the vital roles that trade unions can play in facilitating such transformations/revolutions. Finally, because capitalism is rife with exploitative and volatile outcomes that adversely affect workers and their families and communities, transformation is shown to be not only possible, but also highly desirable.

Although democracy is not necessarily a given in a WSDE class structure, workers and/or their representatives could ensure democratic surplus allocations that could result in a work and social environment that is more congenial to workers and their communities. For example, workers in a WSDE class process could make surplus distributions that support worker-friendly institutions, political policies, and social structures, while withholding distributions that infringe on their expectations. It should be made clear that in the prevailing socioeconomic and political conditions, WSDEs often face adverse, even ravaging circumstances, to which they may succumb. This eventuality is particularly evident when such a firm is in direct competition with a more profitable and more powerful capitalist firm, as was the case with the Lusty Lady. There is much to be learned from this particular case, particularly from the valiant efforts of the Lusties, how they are affectionately known, to persevere and manage for as long as they did. Nonetheless, the probability of success should increase when those who are directly affected by any outcomes are involved in the decision-making processes. Moreover, with worker (and member/community) participation, decisions regarding not only the employees' working conditions, but also their community's economic development and sustainable (environmentally friendly) pursuits might prove superior to the actions of capitalist firms, whose central goal is to maximize profits. For example, the workers will make surplus distributions to secure their conditions of existence not only as WSDE workers, but also to make their living environments and their communities more family- and worker-friendly. The NMCA of the six institutions presented in this volume will provide workers with a roadmap and with suggestions for improving the conditions under which they toil and live.

# CHAPTER 2

# The London Symphony
# Orchestra: Still Afloat

## Introduction

The London Symphony Orchestra (LSO) is my first case study, not only because it is the oldest continuously running self-governed enterprise featured in this book, but also because it is ranked the fourth-greatest orchestra in the world according to the leading magazine in the field, *Gramophone*.[1] In fact, there is no US or UK orchestra ranked higher than the LSO, and it is indeed a Worker Self-Directed Enterprise (WSDE), a little detail that many people no doubt ignore, dismiss, or simply don't know or care to know. The LSO's rich over one-hundred-year history has included multiple domestic and international crises: two world wars, the Great Depression, technological advancements that replace workers, and even Margaret Thatcher. In spite of all these crises and struggles, the LSO is now officially "in the black" and making long-term efforts to remain viable.

I first heard of the LSO's organizational structure while giving a paper at a conference a few years ago and then became fascinated with it; thus I decided to research it further, even spending a month in London speaking to workers, sifting through multiple documents, and working with the orchestra's archivist. After completing my field and academic research, I concluded that this orchestra, with only two minor "infractions" or caveats as I like to call them, is indeed a WSDE within the NMCA methodology. This chapter examines the LSO and its affiliate endeavors, which include its own record label and various other activities that help to secure its conditions of existence.

## The Birth of an Orchestra

The British Proms,[2] one of the world's most eminent symphony orchestra engagements, began in 1895 under the management of Sir Robert Newman, who soon hired Sir Henry Wood as the first conductor of the then "Queen's Hall" orchestra. At the time, Newman was the managing director London's newly constructed Queens Hall (1893), which accommodated an audience of 2,500 people.[3] Newman's goal was to reach a broad audience with the Proms, and he succeeded. However, in the meantime all was not harmonious within the orchestra. The orchestra members were at odds with both Newman and Wood, because the latter reviled the musicians' usual practice of engaging "deputy" (substitute) musicians to take their places during rehearsals and sometimes during concerts. This rift became the catalyst for the establishment of a new orchestra.

On May 19, 1904, Newman and Wood unilaterally issued an edict forbidding the musicians' use of deputies. The deputy system was (and still is) essential to the musicians' livelihoods because among other factors, there was (and still is) rarely enough full-time work in a symphony orchestra to provide an adequate income for musicians. The new edict had dire consequences when four "radical" Queen's Hall musicians, Henri van der Meerschen, Adolf Borsdorf, Thomas Busby, and John Solomon, resigned in protest and were soon followed by others. They despised their employer's dictatorial management practices, and the dispute over deputies had been the last straw. They organized their own democratic, worker-run, self-governed collective orchestra, which became the London Symphony Orchestra (Morrison, 2004, 22).

Deputies (known in the United States as substitutes) replace orchestra members during rehearsals and sometimes during performances, when the permanent musician(s) cannot perform, whether for personal reasons, or, as is more commonly the case, because of more lucrative engagements elsewhere. The management's decision to forbid the use of deputies thus compromised their incomes and their professional reputations as talented and diverse musicians. Then as now, hiring deputies provides musicians with an outlet not only to supplement their typically insufficient incomes, but also to pursue employment that enables them to keep current in professional circles.

On that fateful day in 1904, Robert Newman—considered the Queen's Hall Orchestra's "moneyman"—with the support of the conductor, Henry Wood,[4] simply announced at a rehearsal, at which ironically many deputies were working, that "in the future there will no deputies" (Morrison, 2004, 11). The musicians were outraged; in fact, they thought that Wood and Newman were interfering with "free trade"—very popular in Edwardian and Victorian England—in that their right to sell their services to the highest bidder was being compromised (Morrison, 2004, 13). Thereafter, more than one half of the musicians resigned (Morrison, 2004, 23). In their newly formed orchestra, the LSO, it was of paramount importance *not* to employ a permanent conductor, for fear he would have too much power and/or influence (Foss and Goodwin 1954, 12–13). As to Henry Wood, it seems he tried to ignore the split and anything problematic given his omission of the LSO in his over 450-word autobiography, entitled *My Life of Music* (1938).

It is still true that most conductors and orchestra managers oppose the deputy/substitute practice, arguing that they never know who will playing (working) at any given time, and that this can significantly and negatively affect the outcome of a performance. Management argues, for example, that the conductor might give some nuanced directions during a rehearsal in which the deputy is present, information that might not be passed on to the orchestra member who actually plays the concert. The musicians counter this by pointing out that the deputy makes copious notes and communicates the directions to the member, as is the case with the Broadway musicians, for example. This tension has existed for well over a century and continues in the present in orchestras around the globe (Mulder, 2009).

Ironically, the new members of the self-governed LSO eventually found themselves questioning the use of deputies and found the practice to be quite problematic. Indeed, Carnegie

Hall's executive and artistic director Clive Gillinson, who was the LSO's managing director from 1984 to 2005,[5] proclaimed that the LSO became the "antithesis" of the reason it was founded (Morrison, 2004, 14). The musicians nevertheless retained their self-governance structure and collectively created an alternative system, the "dual principal program" that has solved the deputy problem. This program, which will be discussed in more detail below, it is but one example of how the workers who are directly affected successfully solved a significant problem without the intervention of a CEO or his/her henchmen.

While I do not believe that the musicians who founded the LSO really understood just how revolutionary their actions were, they did in fact organize themselves into a new WSDE, one devoid of any exploitation. With little or no assistance, these musicians were able to form their own enterprise choosing a collaborative path, not a hierarchical one, as was the norm, and unlike many other collective organizations, it has withstood all exogenous pressures to conform. My conversations with the LSO members and staff suggest, however, that the current musicians do not really grasp how unique and progressive their organizational structure is. Their ignorance could be due firstly to the orchestra's longevity; the musicians may simply be unfamiliar with its revolutionary roots. A possibly more compelling reason is that the other three private sector London orchestras are also "self-governing." The workers may not realize how remarkable it is that the LSO has not only survived economic downturns, war, and funding issues, but also retains its non-hierarchical structure within a global capitalist environment.

## The LSO Today

Today, London has four other symphony orchestras in addition to the LSO, and, although many question the need for five world-class orchestras in London, they all somehow manage to exist. They are the London Philharmonic, the Philharmonia, the Royal Philharmonic, and the BBC Symphony Orchestra. Except for the BBC Orchestra, the orchestras are privately controlled and operated, albeit with some public funding. While the four private-sector orchestras are all self-governed, the public BBC Orchestra (which shares symphony space at the Barbican with the LSO) is run as a capitalist enterprise, even though it is non-profit; there is no self-governance or worker democracy (Mulder, 2015). The LSO, with its vast repertoire and many ventures, may well be the most popular. The four LSO founders opted for a democratic and communal organizational structure that remains in place today, albeit on a much grander scale in that they now have a full complement of highly skilled symphony musicians, they are world renowned and are in great demand for many engagements. The orchestra members and their elected leaders make all the decisions, from where the orchestra performs to what is played at a given concert. Many orchestras, for example, play the same pieces for a variety of performances, with unfortunate consequences such as ennui and carpal tunnel syndrome (Mulder, 2009); the LSO has rejected this practice.

Of paramount importance to the LSO founders was the commitment to maintain and implement democratic principles, particularly the notion of one person, one vote, and self-governance, and an ethos that continues today. However, though its current financial situation is sustainable, decreasing audiences and insufficient resources continually challenge the LSO. Although the orchestra's funding relies heavily on state subsidies and wealthy benefactors, it has managed to secure its own longevity thanks to some very creative undertakings.

Its class structure has given the LSO members leeway to be creative not only in their musicianship, but also in securing their conditions of existence. They have overcome difficulties in novel and interesting ways, finding solutions that would probably not have been possible within a capitalist class process. With its longevity and world-class status, the LSO is a quintessential example of a successful worker initiative that counters the popular belief that such structures cannot survive indefinitely or cannot compete within a global, primarily capitalist economy.

It was not until I had delved into the LSO archives in the fall of 2011 and had interviewed particular agents that I realized that the LSO is an almost an entirely a WSDE firm. But while their WSDE economic process is egalitarian, some of the other governance structures (political processes) are far from democratic. For example, the LSO support staff members do not participate in the orchestra's governance structure and are instead the musicians' employees; thus under certain methodological approaches the LSO would not be deemed a cooperative. However, since the support staff are non-productive workers who do not produce surplus, this does not negate the LSO's WSDE class structure within the NMCA. Another important feature of the LSO's governance system is that it does not base its decisions on profit maximization, but rather on worker satisfaction and income security. As I mentioned above, there are two "moments" or caveats that make it impossible to classify the LSO as a purely WSDE: the conductors' and the deputies' positions. While these two caveats make it impossible for us to consider the LSO a perfect WSDE, I will provide suggestions on how these contradictions can be resolved, given that the occupants of both positions produce surplus, but are prohibited from participating in governance. Typically, though, the conductor has a lucrative contract, high stature, power over the music's quality, and much prominence. I am therefore very comfortable excusing this minor issue rather than disregarding the collective and/or democratic structure of the LSO entirely. On the other hand, the deputies do not enjoy the same benefits as the conductors, and this is a much more egregious divergence from the LSO's WSDE class structure. Nonetheless, because today's deputies are often tomorrow's members, they are typically content to participate in this capacity; it is similar to a prolonged audition.

### The London Symphony Orchestra and Its Economic Structure

Self-governance does not necessarily imply an enterprise is a WSDE, that is, one that produces and appropriates surplus as a collective. During my month-long research trip to London, when I interviewed many musicians and employees, I therefore needed to determine whether or not this world-class orchestra is truly self-governed and moreover a WSDE. Additionally, in order to verify the WSDE economic structure, I obtained access to archives at LSO headquarters, which housed the various business meeting minutes, bylaws, and the like. My firsthand research reaffirmed my initial hypothesis that a WSDE is not a utopian dream, but one that is possible and also sustainable.

At its 1904 inception, the orchestra members formed a collective, one in which all members had the same rights, working conditions, and privileges—and these tenets are still observed today. The LSO's *Articles of Association* clearly state that "[t]he Company shall be controlled and its shares held by Performing Members only" (Article 2, LSO). Each LSO member is issued ten shares of stock in the orchestra, at a cost of a mere £1 apiece. These are unlike shares sold on any stock exchange: they cannot be sold on the market, do not offer dividends, their price does not fluctuate with market forces, nor can anyone hold a share who is not a playing member of the LSO. Moreover, shares must be immediately returned when a musician separates from the orchestra for whatever reason. The paper shares are no longer even distributed to the members, but instead are kept on file at the LSO headquarters. There were/are never more than a thousand shares in existence since the LSO always has fewer than one hundred members.

The LSO members elect their own orchestra committees and board of directors, who then choose their own "chairman," currently violinist Lennox McKenzie. The most vital requirement of the chair and the committees is that they must be actively playing (working) members of the orchestra. In the early days of the LSO, the board met quite frequently and truly made every decision; they kept detailed records which still exist in the LSO archives thus, it is evident from them that issues from the most important to the most trivial or mundane were often discussed, debated, and addressed. Indeed, the *Articles of Association* also require monthly meetings of the board. The original board made decisions about such matters as fines imposed on a rogue musician, tour itineraries, the schedule of performances, and the appointment of the managing director and even the conductor(s). Today, the board meets approximately every three weeks and the full orchestra committee meets quarterly. Even though I was not given permission to see the LSO's current meeting minutes, I did conduct extensive interviews with many, and the archived minutes make it clear that the original LSO musicians were absolutely self-governed and democratic. And I can say with a much confidence that self-governance remains the case today. The primary change in governance is that the board now appoints a non-playing business manager (currently Kathryn McDowell) and a non-playing secretary (Rikesh Shah), who run the LSO's daily operations with the help of about sixty staff members. The orchestra's chairman works closely with the business manager to ensure that the musicians' wishes and decisions are carried out. While the business manager and secretary positions are vital and they assume many responsibilities and wield some power, their employment remains at the behest of the orchestra members.

The LSO also has a finance committee, which is chaired by a non-orchestra member who is not an employee, the very wealthy and very well connected entrepreneur, Christopher Moran. This committee also includes the appointed financial director (Moran), three orchestra members, two additional external members, and LSO secretary Rikesh Shah (*ex-officio*). It is significant that until relatively recently, the committee had no external members but was composed solely of elected orchestra members. Today, because the LSO receives funding from the state via the British Arts Council, it is mandated that the committee include three "independent" committee members to avoid potential conflicts of interest. Rather than ceding this much-needed funding, the musicians agreed to the inclusion of the "outsiders" on the finance committee. It should be noted, however, that, if the Arts Council should withdraw its funding, or if the musicians find other funding sources, they can vote to include only orchestra members once again. Members of the LSO staff indicated to me that these external members act primarily in an advisory capacity.

From some theoretical perspectives, the musicians' control over the committees might make problematic their class positions. That is, the elected chair and board, acting for the musicians, can hire and fire not only the conductors, but also the LSO non-member staff, including the management. Indeed, at one point they fired one of their most famous conductors, Maestro Edward Elgar, because of declining box office receipts (Morrison, 2004, 42). According to some schools of economic thought, since the musicians have this power, the LSO would not a true cooperative, given some workers' exclusion. But if the roles are investigated from a surplus-producing NMCA perspective, a very different conclusion is reached. That is, precisely because it is the musicians who produce the surplus, appropriate it, and then make collective decisions on how to allocate it via their democratically elected officials, there is no exploitation. This is the very definition of a WSDE within the NMCA framework. Even though the musicians control the employment of the non-playing workers, from the business manager to the receptionist, who provide much needed support and ensure the success of the LSO's endeavors, the enterprise is indeed a WSDE. The rather subtle difference is that these other workers, no matter how vital they are to the institution by virtue of the essential conditions of existence they provide, do not produce surplus.

## New Marxian Class Analysis of the LSO

The NMCA approach is used in this book to emphasize the class relations between the agents within a particular organization, whether they are privately or publically organized and whether they are non-profit or for-profit enterprises. This analysis enables the reader to get a clear and concise understanding of the intricacies within an organization or enterprise. Even with the two caveats, the LSO is a superb example the richness of the methodology and how changes can be made to make a given enterprise more inclusive. Identifying the LSO musicians' class positions vis-à-vis the other agents within their sphere makes the enterprise structure comprehensible and delineates the various participants' class or non-class positions. Because the "entry point" of every NMCA is "class," two basic questions must be answered: Who produces the surplus? And who appropriates it and distributes it? The LSO workers produce a commodity, in this case music. The musicians receive payments for this work on a per service basis. These payments are made for their necessary labor, and, much like workers in other class structures, they produce an amount greater than necessary, the surplus. In every class structure, surplus is produced; we can identify the structure by determining what is done with it once it has been produced.

Unlike the members of many orchestras, who produce a surplus that is collected by capitalists, the LSO musicians occupy two fundamental class positions; they both produce and appropriate their own surplus (Mulder, 2009). Moreover, because the LSO musicians appropriate the surplus, they also distribute it as they see fit. Like capitalists, they then make distributions/payments to many agents to secure their conditions of existence as surplus appropriators (and producers). The LSO staff, for example, receive a portion of the surplus for their work that supports the musicians' surplus production and appropriation. But although these staff members are vital to the smooth operations of the LSO and ensure that the orchestra remains in operation, they do not produce or appropriate surplus, and therefore hold no fundamental class positions. Instead, because they receive a portion of the surplus, they occupy subsumed class positions as surplus recipient. Precisely because the surplus producers also collectively appropriate it, the mode of production is thus democratic and a nearly perfect example of a true WSDE.

## The Two Caveats

There are two caveats that prevent the LSO from being a 100-percent WSDE. This is not surprising. When using any methodology or theoretical approach in an actual case study, rather than as a prototype or model, one frequently discovers that not every aspect fits neatly within it. The two positions that prevent the LSO from being a purely WSDE firm are the two surplus-producing positions that do not participate in the appropriation and distribution of the surplus: the conductor and the deputies. Both positions are occupied by productive workers who do not participate in surplus appropriation and/or distribution. At the same time, the occupants of these two positions, especially the conductor, are essential for the LSO's conditions of existence.

### The Conductor

The first caveat is the conductor's position; within the NMCA framework, the conductor is thus a productive worker who does not occupy the fundamental class position as appropriator and is an exploited worker. In *Capital,* Volume 3, Marx was quite specific about an orchestra conductor's productive position as the coordinator of the music. He stated:

> [I]n all labour where many individuals cooperate, the interconnection and unity of the process is necessarily represented in a governing will, and in functions that concern not the detailed work but rather the workplace and its activity as a whole, as with the conductor of an orchestra. This is productive labour that has to be performed in any combined mode of production. (507)

LSO conductors do not hold shares nor do they participate as collective members; as a result, they are prohibited from holding a position on any orchestra committee or on the board of directors. Because of this prohibition, the conductors, like the musicians, occupy the fundamental class position of surplus producer, but do not appropriate the surplus as the musicians do. Therefore, the conductors do not occupy the second fundamental class position of surplus appropriator, and within the NMCA methodology, the musicians therefore exploit the conductor; however, given his prestige, creative control, and leadership responsibilities, not to mention his extraordinary salary, I am persuaded that we can overlook this small caveat for now and focus on the conditions of existence that the musicians now enjoy. Practically speaking, the orchestra is a WSDE. NMCA, like all theoretical approaches, has its weaknesses, thus giving researchers the opportunity to rethink their methodologies and arrive at an alternative way of analyzing certain positions. Moreover, given the great number of technological changes within the music industry, many argue that a conductor is superfluous. Indeed, in many jazz orchestras and in some of the formerly Soviet symphony orchestras, just to name two examples, the music is either self-conducted or conducted by a playing musician.

The LSO's current conductor is the world renowned Valery Gergiev, who typically signs three-year contracts with the orchestra. However, it was recently announced that Sir Simon Rattle will lead the LSO in September 2015 and Gergiev will be conducting in Munich, Germany.[6] Additionally, the orchestra employs many guest conductors, none of whom appropriates any surplus. However, the conductors hold a subsumed class position of surplus recipients because they receive salaries and benefits above their necessary wages.

### The Deputies

The second caveat is much more problematic, and that is the LSO deputies' positions. These musicians substitute for the collective member musicians who choose for a variety of reasons to absent themselves during either rehearsals or performances, for example to perform in a more lucrative engagement. Obviously, the deputies produce the same commodity as the member musicians next to them. Deputies, however, own no shares and have no control over the surplus. They are not even considered permanent employees of the LSO. Within the NMCA framework, they hold the fundamental class position as surplus producers, yet like the conductors, they do not hold the other fundamental class position of appropriator. Unlike the conductors, they typically do not hold a subsumed class position receiving any premiums; they receive only the necessary wages for their services. Thus, the deputies are also exploited workers, in both the NMCA sense and in the more usual sense, given their precarious work arrangements: they are quite vulnerable and can be fired at any time by the musicians.

It is possible for the deputies to become part of the collective and thus occupy the second fundamental class position as appropriator. The deputies are included on a roster of acceptable substitutes from which the member musicians may choose, and thus they are not unknown and have already been deemed acceptable. The deputies could become partial LSO members, with their share allotment relative to their playing time. That is, the deputies would have partial shares, and their voices would be heard, whether through a vote or some other means, but only in proportion to how much they work.

Accounting and allocating proportional shares seems burdensome, but it would take something like this plan to make the

LSO a completely WSDE. Given the arduous procedures that would be required, perhaps the status quo is acceptable, even though it makes the LSO more of a hybrid class enterprise than a perfect example of a WSDE. Since deputies choose to work in the LSO, one might say that they choose to be exploited. It is likely that they choose this option, hoping that they may one day become permanent members of the LSO; this is in fact the usual avenue for membership in the LSO. It is quite similar to a prolonged audition or interview. The deputy process enables the member musicians not only to judge the quality of the deputies' work, but also allows the members to get to know the deputies and decide whether they would be good colleagues. One often hears, whether on Broadway or in other orchestras, that today's deputies are tomorrow's members. Thus the deputies might be willing to be exploited for the short term, but look forward to the time when they are not.

## The Benefits of the LSO's Structure

Besides the obvious benefit of having a true voice in their working conditions, the LSO musicians and their staff also enjoy a variety of benefits not typically given in a top-down capitalist enterprise. Firstly, the musicians enjoy true job security; that is, there are clear "rules and regulations" that all the musicians have agreed and voted upon, regarding not only their responsibilities, but also the repercussions if these are not met. Firing and hiring decisions are neither arbitrary nor capricious. There are differences of opinion, but somehow for over 110 years, the musicians have "sorted them out."

Secondly, the current players choose the new members, usually from the ranks of the aforementioned deputies. Having played with the orchestra as a deputy is a benefit to both the potential new member and to the orchestra. But the member musicians can also arrange open auditions if that is their preference.

Thirdly, the musicians have voted themselves a health-care benefit that a typical capitalist employer would not provide. As we know, the United Kingdom has a national health program that is available to all its citizens. I understand from anecdotal information I gathered while in London that the NH program has greatly improved, and patients no longer have to wait as long to see a doctor as they once did. Nevertheless, the LSO musicians have decided to supplement the NH program with additional private insurance, which is available to all its members and staff. Many have opted to take advantage of this very generous benefit because it allows them more choice in practitioners, and they can often see doctors sooner than would otherwise be possible. Some have chosen not to participate in the private program for two primary reasons: the first is that, although there is no charge to the musician or staff member for the private coverage, the benefit is taxable as income. The second reason is that some LSO members have the strong ideological belief that health care should be public and equal and that private insurance puts the orchestra on the slippery slope to the privatizing of health care that we have in the United States.

Fourthly, the musicians have come up with a novel approach to the deputy issue. Recall that the original four musicians left the Queen's Hall orchestra because of the new initiative that prohibited the use of deputies. This problem has not ceased to exist, and the LSO musicians have been compelled to find a solution. The deputy process was simultaneously revered and despised until relatively recently. Many believed that the deputies did not meet the same standards as the members, particularly in regard to the principal players—and this issue remained problematic. To address this, the musicians decided to divide the principal chairs into two positions; this became known as the "dual principal" program and is essentially a job-sharing program. Today, there are two principals for each major section of the orchestra. The principals decide in advance which of them will be at each performance, but one or the other of them must be in the chair. Additionally, the non-principal players must notify the orchestra well in advance of the performances for which they will require deputies. The deputies are then hired from a list compiled by the orchestra members. This novel approach, a collective solution to an ongoing problem, seems to have satisfied all concerned.

### Ensuring the Future of the LSO

One very interesting aspect of the London Symphony Orchestra is their collective decision to secure their future conditions of existence with an investment into prospective audiences and musicians. Specifically, the LSO has developed two programs, LSO Discovery and LSO St. Luke's. Discovery is a concerted effort and commitment by the LSO to support music education. An award-winning program that reaches over 60,000 people annually, LSO Discovery provides family concerts and makes substantial investments in young musicians locally, nationally, and internationally. LSO St. Luke's is a music education center, housed only a few short blocks from LSO headquarters in a restored old church that was once in ruins, without so much as a roof. Children and adults may not only take classes at St. Luke's, but they also can attend recitals, lunchtime concerts, and dance and folk music performances, and finally, it is another venue where the orchestra can rehearse. The musicians view these as long-term investments, and in a time of austerity that has witnessed the elimination of music and the arts in both public and private schools, they believe that this will keep people interested in classical music and secure the orchestra's future aspirations. Unlike a typical capitalist enterprise, the LSO's horizon is not the next quarter, or even the next five years, but one that is truly enduring.

The LSO has partnered with the Barbican Centre and the Guildhall School to develop a model program uniting the arts with higher education. According to their publicity material, the Centre for the Orchestra (the LSO's first major undertaking), gives young orchestra musicians unparalleled access to training and development, and at the same time lays the groundwork for the future of the orchestra. Clearly, they are teaching and training their future members!

Then there is LSO-Live, the orchestra's own record label. The LSO performances are recorded and then sold as compact discs, and even electronically for MP3 players. This is yet another example of an investment to assure the longevity of the orchestra. The LSO has also been hired to record music for major motion pictures and for classic rock albums and other musical endeavors.

For example, the LSO was hired to play for one of the most popular Academy Award–winning movies within the last half century, George Lucas's 1977 blockbuster, *Star Wars*. The LSO was subsequently hired to record the soundtrack for six more *Star Wars* films. What the *Star Wars* executives may not have realized is that they commissioned a WSDE to do this work, thereby giving us a prime example of a market transaction between a basically WSDE and a capitalist firm. The point here is that markets can and do exist within a WSDE structure—simply being market driven does not define capitalism or any other class structure.

Having had a chance to do some of my research at the LSO headquarters at the Barbican, I can assure you that it is usually a happy, vibrant office, where many activities are carried out simultaneously, from fundraising and marketing to scheduling of tours, budgeting and payroll, archiving, and preparing for galas—and even accommodating the royals when they attend performances. Witnessing such an operation first hand and discussing a variety of responsibilities with the staff, I observed that these dedicated people truly seem to enjoy their positions; the atmosphere is very different from what I have witnessed in many capitalist workplaces. Every staff member seems quite dedicated to the LSO and its quality of music, and, moreover, they hold the musicians in high esteem. The camaraderie is astounding. For example, a £4,000 donation check came in, and there was a celebration in which everyone participated. I attribute the pleasant atmosphere in the main office to the WSDE structure in which the "management" (i.e., the managing director and the secretary/financial manager) lack absolute power. There is really a sense of community and respect throughout.

### The London Symphony Orchestra and the Musicians' Union

In my previous book (Mulder, 2009) I discussed how the musicians' union in the United States, specifically in New York City, could facilitate change in the enterprise structure from capitalist to a democratic WSDE. The role of the UK musicians' union with regard to the LSO is much different. The union negotiates minimum scale wages with the orchestral trade association, the Association of British Orchestras (ASO). The LSO members' wages are typically higher than the minimum scale wages negotiated, but this wage provides a benchmark for the payments to the musicians for their work. Interestingly enough, Kathryn McDowell, the LSO's appointed business manager, sits on the board of the ABO.

The role of the musicians' union in the LSO is minimal at best; the individual musician can decide whether or not to join the union, although in fact most do seem to be union members. The LSO has its own bylaws, articles of association, rules, standards, and penalties, and the orchestra members themselves make decisions; there is no need to negotiate with management as within a capitalist structure. I've often heard that unions have outlived their usefulness, and perhaps when transformations from capitalist enterprises to WSDEs become more widespread—that is, when there is a class revolution—this may prove to be true.

## The LSO: Final Thoughts

It is unlikely that those four musicians in 1904 were trying to start a revolution; they simply knew that they wanted fair working conditions. Yet the LSO has survived two world wars, the Blitz, the Great Depression, many recessions, and frequent large deficits, and it remains one of the world's most prominent symphony orchestras. The LSO has regrouped and has been able to do so relatively quickly, given that the members can institute changes at a moment's notice as they deem necessary. In the last few years, funding from private sources, for the LSO as for many charities, has become scarcer, but the orchestra has managed to remain solvent; it has not been in arrears since the 1980s. The LSO shows us clearly that workers, even creative types who more than likely did not take very many finance courses in college can be and are successful in running their own enterprises. The idea that there must be visionary CEOs who have made their own financial investment in the enterprise, and that capitalism is the most efficient and desirable enterprise structure, is quite simply bunk.

One final note regarding the phrase "Still Afloat" in the title of this chapter: in 1912 the London Symphony Orchestra was scheduled to tour the United States and had booked passage on the ill-fated *Titanic*. Luckily, the orchestra was given the opportunity to expand its US tour, and thus passage was booked on the *HMS Baltic*, sailing two weeks earlier. . . .

# CHAPTER 3

# Capitalism's Triumph: The Case of the Lusty Lady

As the title of this chapter indicates, capitalism did indeed triumph in the case of the strip club/peep show, the Lusty Lady, but not without a fight. The Lusty Lady workers were extremely devoted to being both a cooperative and unionized. In fact, one of the former dancers, Lily Burana wrote a piece for *The Atlantic* that sums up how they felt, she said:

> To many of us, dancers, patrons, and support staff alike, the closing of the Lusty Lady means not just the demise of a singular San Francisco institution, but another nail in the coffin of the Bay Area's Bohemian class—a triumph of capitalism over native culture. The way of all things in this town, it appears, at least for now. So, Lusty Lady, as we must, we surrender you to the ages and to the clutches of big business. Oh, sweet Lady, you dive, you dreambox, you were something special. You will be missed. (2013)

Transcending capitalism is often a difficult task, no matter how much effort and dedication the workers put into it. Unlike the London Symphony Orchestra, the Lusty Lady, which made a valiant attempt to be a self-governed worker cooperative failed finally on Labor Day in 2013. The closing of what had become a San Francisco institution was not due to internal struggles or the common anecdotal grumblings about the need for a leader, someone in charge who makes sure the workers do their jobs efficiently and effectively.

As we saw with the LSO, a leader/supervisor is not a mandatory requirement for a successful enterprise. Indeed, as I write this book, more and more firms are looking for capitalist alternatives—because the system is failing many of them. Nonetheless, monopoly power and an environment that embraces a capitalist culture, norms, laws, and business practices can have dire effects on small cooperatives that are simply trying to eke out a living. In NMCA terms, the conditions of existence for such a collective enterprise are continually compromised. This was the case with the Lusty Lady.

When I began my research for this book, "the Lusty" was not exactly thriving, but it was at least sustainable. The enterprise, however, seemed to meet with adversity at every stage of its development. This may have been because of the type of firm it was and the industry in which it existed, or more likely because the Lusty Lady was a threat to the monopolization of the industry by Déjà Vu Consulting, Inc. Clearly, the Lusty "experiment" was a failure, but the question of why it failed remains to be answered. Simply blaming the hegemonic Déjà Vu Corporation does not sufficiently explain the constant attacks and hardships these workers endured. There is much to learn from the Lusty's experiences, and by using the NMCA methodology, we can validate their efforts and gain an appreciation for the Lusty's almost ten-year tenure as the only worker-cooperative in the sex-entertainment industry.

## Discovery and My Journey to San Francisco

Between the years 1999 and 2002, I was a visiting instructor in economics at Franklin & Marshall College in Lancaster, Pennsylvania. While there, I was given the opportunity to develop my own courses, one of which was a class called Labor and Film. The class focused each week on a specific labor topic—labor history, workplace discrimination, collective bargaining, and others. Various readings and films that complemented them were assigned to encourage the students to think about labor issues. What made this class unique was that I did not simply use films considered the old standards, no matter how wonderful. I found movies where nobody else would look—Disney and Pixar's *A Bug's Life*, for instance, a very good example of workers and class revolution (Mulder, 2013). Finding a good film for collective bargaining was a bit more difficult than for some of the other topics. Of course, there are union-produced documentaries; but these films were in my view boring and sophomoric. Then I came across a film entitled *Live Nude Girls Unite*, which offered a compelling depiction of a union's organizing efforts and the collective-bargaining process.

The film, directed and written by Vicky Funari and Julia Query, depicts the journey of the Lusty Lady to unionization and a first collective-bargaining agreement. It is a documentary discussing the problems that the workers faced, such as discrimination, shift changes, working conditions, and, in particular, unauthorized filming of the dancers by customers. What really struck me as I watched the film was the fact that these workers confronted many of the same issues that workers in other industries face; they simply happened to be in an industry that challenges the ethics and morals of many people.

Moreover, the film shows that from a feminist perspective there are at least two ways of thinking about these workers: on the one hand, many feminists believe that the sex industry demeans women and is the ultimate form of exploitation. As Tad Friend says in a 2004 *New Yorker* article: "Traditionally, stripping is capitalism at its most explicit: men sell women's bodies to other men. The idea behind the new Lusty Lady was that capitalism would give way to the utopian glories of self-ownership" (56). But that is only one way of thinking about these workers. Women who work in the sex-entertainment industry are in fact *workers*, and they choose to be in this business for a variety of reasons. They produce a commodity, a service that is consumed by its patrons. As one worker put it: "[W]e produce assembly line orgasms."[1] Most of the customers were men, but sometimes women and couples were among the Lusty's patrons, and most of them came to masturbate. During my one-hour chat with the Lusty's CFO, who was manning the entrance in 2013, I watched one of the cleaning staff continually changing her gloves after cleaning each booth when the patron departed.

*Live Nude Girls Unite*, released in 2000, is a primer that clearly spells out the ABCs of union organizing in general and the collective-bargaining process in particular, emphasizing how arduous such a process is, especially the drawing up of a first contract. In the film, there was a simultaneous backstory about the relationship of Julia Query, one of the film's authors, with her mother, interesting because it emphasizes the differing views of feminists regarding sex work.[2] "[T]he film advocates a solution through the cooperative enterprise of labor organizing, which represents the socialist hope and political possibilities that feminist solidarity can effect. More important, this film informs spectators that the potential for feminist praxis and collective action still exists." (Borda, 2009, 120). The film also emphasizes how workers address and take action against rogue employers and the necessity of being not only creative in their approaches to work slowdowns or stoppages, but also in being industry specific. For example, one of the Lusty workers' rallying cries while picketing and asking potential customers not to enter the Lusty was "two, four, six, eight, don't come here to masturbate" (ibid.). While, according to Borda, some "conservative" onlookers (both men and women) thought the workers had moral reasons for their protest, their rallying cry did receive much attention, as did some of the posters. (One poster proclaimed that "Bad Girls Like Good Contracts"— which of course was the workers' goal [ibid.].)

It was the film that piqued my interest in sex-entertainment workers, especially the Lusty workers. Most of the dancers had post-graduate degrees, including some PhDs. Moreover, when they were wronged, they decided to change their working conditions and ultimately formed their own cooperative, self-governed enterprise. In order to truly appreciate how diligent, proud, and tenacious these workers were—and how regrettable it is that their enterprise failed—one needs to know a bit more of the Lusty's history. As we will see, capitalist obstacles had much to do with the Lusty's fate.

### The Lusty's History

Given the uniqueness and possibly also the allure of discussing a somewhat taboo subject, there are a plethora of historical accounts of the Lusty Lady, and I will simply provide a short overview and summary of the literature here. The San Francisco Lusty Lady first opened in 1976 on Kearny Street in San Francisco's North Bay area, once known as the Barbary Coast, having been incorporated as the Multivue Incorporated on September 29, 1975 (The Articles of Incorporation).[3] Seattle, Washington already had a similar business with the same name and ownership. A small establishment in what many would call a "seedy" neighborhood, it first opened as a theater showing 16-mm pornographic films, but then, in 1983, the Lusty's management decided to hire live "exotic dancers," and thus it became a peep show as well. Patrons, typically men, would enter a private booth and put money in a slot, a one-way window would open to a separate small room with mirrors and a stage, where the naked or scantily clad ladies danced, stripped, and performed other forms of exotic adult entertainment.

As is the case in many capitalist workplaces, the management consistently attempted, usually successfully, to treat the workers as they deemed fit. However, by 1996, the Lusties (their self-imposed name) became incensed with management's often arbitrary and capricious practices, much as the LSO musicians had done. Like the LSO musicians, the Lusties required substitutes from time to time and for various reasons (additional work, school, childcare, menstruation, etc.). The Lusty managers, however, insisted that a substitute have the same body type, hair color, and image as the worker she replaced, which often forced the women to come to work, even when it was extremely problematic to do so. This practice became overtly discriminatory and often left women of color or women with small breasts without enough shifts to make a living.[4] Because the windows were one-way glass, the dancers could not see the patrons, but they could see red lights from video cameras, which were supposedly not permitted. Additionally, although there was a one- or two-customer limit per booth, the doors were often left open so that more customers could peep, a practice that amounted to the theft of the commodities produced by the dancers. These were the complaints and issues that the workers found intractable. Unlike the LSO musicians, however, instead of quitting and forming their own enterprise, the dancers and the staff had by 1997 organized themselves and had brought in the Service Employees International Union (SEIU) to advise and represent them.

As is frequently the case with a union organizing drive, management tried strenuously to obstruct it. The efforts of the dancers and support staff did succeed, but only after protests, slow-downs, and the like. Eventually, a collective-bargaining agreement negotiated, albeit one with many concessions by the workers. The documentary *Live Nude Girls Unite* details the pitfalls and tribulations of negotiating and signing a first collective-bargaining agreement (contract). Having been a union member and an elected union officer myself, I know that concluding a first contract/collective-bargaining agreement is difficult, not only because of the lack of experience on both labor and management sides, but also because management is forced to cede some of its power.

Though many often refer to the Lusty as the first unionized peep show, it was not. Pacers, a strip club in San Diego, was the first, represented by the Hotel Employees and Restaurant Employees union (HERE). The workers, though, agreed to an "open shop," one in which there is no requirement for the workers to join the union or pay union dues, unlike the "agency" shop that is negotiated in most unionized workplaces. The basic problem with this arrangement is that dues are the only legal source of revenue that US unions can receive. Conversely though, unions are required by law to represent all workers, even the non-dues-paying, non-members, including but not limited to bargaining, grievance handling, and organizing new members. By recruiting workers who promised not to join the union, the management was able to break the union very quickly in the 1990s.[5] Knowing what had happened at Pacers, the Lusty workers demanded an "agency" shop, one in which all members of the bargaining unit pay dues, whether or not they join the union. The Lusties failed in this effort, but they did reach a compromise with a "maintenance of membership" clause in their first collective-bargaining agreement. This clause basically states that, once workers become union members, they must remain so for the duration of the collective-bargaining agreement. The Lusty workers agreed to this and they remained unionized until the club's demise.

*Live Nude Girls Unite* provides us with an excellent account of the Lusties' initial organizing efforts, thus I need not tell their story in detail here because the film is readily available. However, I got the opportunity to interview some Lusty workers and a union representative during a research trip to San Francisco and subsequently via telephone and Skype. What I learned was just how dedicated these workers were to their jobs, the success of the cooperative, and just how much the Lusty meant to them.

## Becoming Unionized Workers

From the very start of their union-organizing drive, the workers at the Lusty faced many problems, not only from their employer, but by established unions as well. Unlike most union-organizing drives, the Lusties organized themselves first and then sought out a formal union, many of which, for a variety of reasons, declined to represent them—for example, the possibility of being associated with organized crime (Wilmet, 1998, n. 196). Eventually, however, the SEIU recognized that these workers faced many of the same problems as workers in other crafts/industries, and helped them organize their own local, 790, the "exotic dancers" local. After many long, tense negotiating sessions, Multivue, Inc. (management), and Local 790, SEIU, signed their first agreement on April 4, 1997 (Kuntz, 1997, E7). The first collective-bargaining agreement did not include all the dancers' demands, but the first contract did spell out wages, bonuses, breaks, a non-discrimination clause, the elimination of the one-way windows, and even forbade sexual harassment. Like most first collective-bargaining agreements, it was very short, but it was a start. What the unionization drive did accomplish was to create some harmony between the dancers and the support staff that had not existed previously.

Between 1997 and 2003, the club struggled financially because of the advent of Internet pornography. In a telephone interview with one of the dancers, "Delinqua" (her stage name),[6] I learned that collective bargaining in such a precarious environment was arduous and that, even though the workers agreed to wage concessions, they were notified in February 2003 that the Lusty would close by May of that year (Delinqua, telephone conversation with author, February 17, 2013). According to Delinqua, fellow dancer Cayenne saw the notice posted and warned the others; they were all very upset. Thus began the spontaneous forging of wildcat strikes. Although they had some support from the SEIU, the workers felt like outcasts (in Delinqua's words, like the "redheaded step-child"). That is, the workers signed a new collective-bargaining agreement in February 2013 that included a no strike/no lockout clause. Any sanctioning of wildcat strikes by the SEIU would have been detrimental and illegal; the union would in fact have been subject to a lawsuit. The workers may not have understood the union's position, which exemplifies one of the constraints under which unions work in the United States. The workers decided after much discussion that they would not allow the Lusty to simply close. Indeed, in one meeting, Delinqua made a motion that there should be "no surrender—fight." And that is what they did. They decided to purchase and operate the Lusty themselves. The union, while supportive, was used only as a "resource"; "the girls were it," Delinqua said, "—it's on us."

## Becoming a Cooperative

The Lusty workers wanted to purchase the firm and also to remain unionized, more for symbolic reasons than for any other, according to Delinqua; then they faced the real issue of finding the financing to purchase the Lusty. Since the only collateral they had was their ability to work—that is, to sell their labor power—and since lenders consider this a non-tangible asset, they were denied financing. The workers finally made a deal with the former owners to hold the note, promising to pay the mortgage in full within five years. The price for the business, not including the building, was $400,000 (Burana, 2014, 3). The workers were successful in paying the note within this time, but to their dismay, the landlord raised their rent by precisely the same amount as their monthly mortgage payments.

Like any other organization, though the internal dynamics were not without some problems and struggles over a variety of issues, particularly when faced with so many external assaults on their cooperative. Even with these exogenous pressures, the Lusty somehow endured. As it says on its website, "Although worker ownership is a rare and ideal situation, it is not without its challenges . . . . And if we want something done . . . we have to do it ourselves. But the beauty of it is, we do."[7] But then everything changed when the building that housed the Lusty was sold and the new landlord was their major competitor, who was accused of monopolistic behavior, but has not, to date, been legally challenged for it.

In 1998, Roger Forbes, a Nevada real-estate tycoon, known in some circles as the "Porn King," bought the building that housed the Lusty, along with other businesses (Sward et al., 1997). Forbes immediately raised the rent from $5,500 to $13,500 a month, a change of almost 150 percent. Within the next decade, he increased the rent again, this time by $3,000 (ibid.). One of the key reasons the original owners had for selling the Lusty to the workers was that the rent increases had made their enterprise unprofitable. With revenues waning, the high rent was prohibitive for the Lusty cooperative members, too, but somehow the Lusties made the cooperative model work. Every one of the approximately 85 Lusty workers who chose to do so could buy into the cooperative for $300, an amount that could be paid through payroll deductions or in one lump sum.

The cooperative's legal name was the Looking Glass Cooperative, incorporated as a domestic nonprofit enterprise with the State of California on May 1, 2003. The members had very specific bylaws and an operations manual that spelled out in detail the roles and responsibilities of all the workers. The first sentence of the bylaws states that "[t]he Corporation shall have one class of members" (Looking Glass Collective, 2003, 1.01). Their goal was that all workers, whether performers or support staff, would have the same opportunities and working conditions as their colleagues. Job descriptions for both categories were detailed and made extremely clear to all the workers. Within the NMCA methodology, such delineation is imperative; that is, the job descriptions of those who are actually producing surplus value are differentiated from the job descriptions of those who ensure its realization. But both categories were members of the collective. The Looking Glass Cooperative was different, then, from the London Symphony Orchestra because it permitted all the workers to become members of the collective, unlike the LSO, which only allowed surplus producing workers to be members.

Lusty workers could become cooperative members after a 90-day probationary period. Worker-members were required to attend meetings, for which they were paid according to the negotiated union collective-bargaining agreement. All members were entitled to one vote, no matter what their seniority or position. Members elected their board of directors, Madams (chairs), and all committees. An individual member was permitted to be on only one elected board at any time, so that power would be "shared." All members were paid according to the multiplier set by the collective-bargaining agreement, and they received payments for any additional work they did in their roles as a representative of the cooperative. In the next chapter, which deals with New Era Cooperative, we will encounter a challenge to the conventional "us versus them" labor/management scenario: the workers are both management and labor, and this sometimes forces them to become quite creative in how they approach various problems, issues, and organizational structure.

The mission statement of the Looking Glass Cooperative is unique and deserves to be acknowledged; it underscores and exemplifies the ability, warmth, and intelligence of these workers who are so readily marginalized. It states:

> We the members of the Looking Glass Cooperative strive to establish and maintain a positive work environment embracing equality and individuality. We view each worker/owner as a unique and important component in our efforts and appreciate the participation of all members in every contribution towards this goal. We extinguish the concept of hierarchy and provide a division of labor based upon a system of equality, promoting greater opportunities to expand upon our roles and develop a variety of skills. With the challenges that we face, it is imperative that all members make distinct efforts to communicate, maintain an open-mindedness to diversity, and respect the needs of the cooperative as well as all members. (Looking Glass Collective, Operations Manual)

As I have previously stated, the Looking Glass Cooperative was officially established as a non-profit corporation on May 1, 2003, with the State of California. The previous owner, Multivue, Inc., was a for-profit enterprise originally incorporated on September 29, 1975. Then on January 20, 2011, Multivue, Inc., officially filed for non-profit status and changed its name to the Multivue *Cooperative*, Inc. The collective-bargaining agreements were then between Multivue Cooperative and SEIU. I believe the change was made because of the limitations of the National Labor Relations Act, according to which supervisors are prohibited from unionizing. I point this out for those who might want to look further into the legalities, and to emphasize that laws can sometimes impede the formation of some types of cooperative organization.

All members of the cooperative were (in theory) treated equally. Even though there was one "class" of workers according to their operations manual (OM), there were in fact two types of workers—performers and support staff. The Lusty's bylaws and OM acknowledged the differences and took them into account. For example, to prevent ennui and exhaustion, dancers had 10-minute breaks every hour and had shorter shifts than the support staff. On the other hand, the support staff worked a more traditional schedule. The cooperative's bylaws acknowledge and list detailed responsibilities for the leaders of both types of workers, Madams of the House for the dancers and "Lead Team" for the support staff.

The elected leaders ran the everyday operations; the Madams supervised the performers, and the Support Staff Lead Team the janitors, cashiers, technicians, bookkeeping, and accounting. The leaders worked at the behest of the board members, who ultimately were under the entire cooperative's rule. As stated above, the workers were paid according to the collective-bargaining agreement with the SEIU; however, any additional net revenues (what the bylaws term "surplus") were divided among the workers according to a democratically devised system, the primary criterion of which was seniority.

The board of directors was an elected body of seven workers, with two positions reserved for support staff. Directors, who were elected for a one-year term in two separate, staggered elections, had some limited incoming and outgoing transitional training. Each of them had a specific responsibility that included two secretaries, two finance officers, two theater coordinators, and a membership liaison. All decisions, however, were made at quarterly meetings of all members of the cooperative.

## The Cooperative's Demise

Roger Forbes and his business partner Harry V. Mohney, known as the "Howard Hughes of Porn," own the Déjà Vu Consulting, which runs and owns more than 80 "adult-oriented businesses" in 14 states (Sward, et al., 1997). In fact, Mohney, later together with Forbes, began buying up many of the strip clubs/ adult-entertainment clubs in San Francisco's North Beach area. The San Francisco clubs were bought up so quickly that they were often referred to as "McStrip" clubs, or, as Delinqua put it, the "Walmart" of the adult-entertainment industry. Only Forbes's name appears on all the San Francisco clubs, and Mohney has been successful in evading notoriety, even among the authorities, although it is against California law to have "silent partners" in these types of clubs to keep them "as clean as they can" (ibid.). It is not certain who really owns the land or the clubs, but most of the documentation I have seen has them linked one way or another.[8] The mystery surrounding ownership of the clubs has no particular bearing on the analysis that follows; I simply want to indicate that the Lusty workers did not always have complete and accurate information, which made their work environment even more miasmic than it would otherwise have been.

During my research trip to the Lusty in January of 2013, I sensed that the business was in some kind of difficulty. The Madam refused to talk with me, even though I had given her sufficient notice. I did, however, speak to some of the dancers, the financial secretary, some support staff, and a union representative. From them, I learned that negotiations were going on behind the scenes. The workers were even asking locals and regulars for donations, just to have adequate funds for payroll. Additionally, according to Fred,[9] a former union representative, the Lusties were at the time in negotiations with the SEIU to change the "successor clause" in their collective-bargaining agreement, a clear signal to me that something was amiss. And indeed, the successor clause (Article 18) had been significantly changed from the previous three-year agreement. In the 2011–2013 contract, there was language about the possibility that the Lusty Lady might cease to be a cooperative. The requisite termination warning was also decreased from sixty days to thirty days. The Lusty's demise was imminent.

The situation became so dire that the Lusties brought in Scott "Big Red" Farrell to help them negotiate the terms of the lease—a questionable decision, given that his qualifications were limited at best. Nevertheless, according to SF Weekly reporter Rachel Swan, when he was made aware of the Lusty's plight, he wanted to help. He believed the "Lusty Lady needed a competent manager to refurbish its digs and parlay with its landlord." (Swan, 2013). Farrell was particularly critical of the Lusty's organization and wanted to disband its self-governing, cooperative model. He wanted a "more traditional business structure"; in other words, he wanted the Lusty to be a capitalist enterprise.

Mr. Farrell's attempts to renegotiate the monthly rental fees with Mr. Forbes failed. Farrell wanted to be a hero, a benefactor who would save the Lusty—but it was not to be. In a telephone interview with Rachel Swan, Forbes said "I'd given them discounts on rent before . . . [b]ut I was tired. It had nothing to do with the rent really. There was no one in charge." Mr. Forbes began eviction proceedings in May, 2013, but (ironically enough) allowed the Lusty to remain open until Labor Day, September 2, 2013. In the meantime, Farrell and the Lusties tried valiantly to win their battle with Forbes, whose reputation as a "hatchet man" in the adult-entertainment business proved to be well deserved. The Lusties fired Farrell and the business finally succumbed in late August. The club was closed on September 2, 2013, as planned.

The Lusty Lady's website remains open today, proudly displaying both its labor history and its former services. The enterprise lasted for a decade, but faced with the many barriers to remaining afloat, they had no alternative but to say goodbye—which they did in a big way. These workers challenged capitalism head on, but the conditions of existence, particularly the cultural, political, and economic barriers, were simply too formidable. My research indicates that their union, the SEIU, did not provide the assistance that these self-governed workers needed; the National Labor Relations Act and the usual role of unions as perennial opponents of management was at least in part to blame for this.

### NMCA and the Lusty Lady

The Lusty found its way into the media, first in 1997 because it was a unionized shop in an industry where unionization is essentially nonexistent. Second, the excellent documentary *Live Nude Girls Unite* popularized the workers' plight in organizing and getting a first contract. Third, it became a collective or a move toward a Worker Self-Directed Enterprise (WSDE) in 2003—an idea that came solely from within the ranks of the workers. And finally, the media covered the closing of the Lusty Lady on Labor Day, 2013. But their story—both the good and the bad experiences they had—can be instructive.

The Lusty Lady has much in common with the London Symphony Orchestra; however, there are some significant differences that may have contributed to the failure of the business. For one thing, the LSO has the advantage of longevity and a cooperative organization model that is the norm in the United Kingdom. Indeed, four of the five London orchestras are self-governed, and the LSO's conditions of existence are thus relatively secure. The Lusty's circumstances were much different; the workers encountered barriers from the very start, particularly when they tried to raise the funds necessary to purchase the theater.

Second, the US labor laws posed another obstacle for Lusty workers: the National Labor Relations Act prohibits management from unionizing. The US business environment also typically favors landlords and moneylenders, two more political realities that compromised the Lusty's existence. Furthermore, there seems to be no ongoing investigation of the questionable monopoly-like practices of Forbes and Mohney, who are buying or have bought most of the property that houses strip clubs and peep shows in various states.

Finally, the LSO is culturally more "acceptable" to the morals and ethics of most people, even of feminists. The portrayed sleaziness of the sex-entertainment industry does not lend itself to conjuring mass appeal and worker support. On the other hand, the performers at the Lusty Lady, like the LSO musicians, are in the entertainment industry, doing a job that many believe is not really "work"; they "play" or "dance" for a living, which does not seem to be "real work," like building a ship or performing a surgical procedure. Yet in fact, they had more in common with other workers than one might expect. It is worth noting that most of the Lusty workers were single mothers, college graduates, or graduate students working on their PhDs; they were by no means a group of amoral women and men as is often assumed.

Like the LSO musicians, the Lusty dancers held fundamental class positions as performers of surplus labor. Also, as is the case with the LSO, these performers were the *direct* or first recipients of any surplus produced. Thus, they also held the fundamental class position of surplus appropriator, and the class process was not exploitative but rather collective—or, in other words, a WSDE. As Farrell and Forbes discovered, there were no bosses, but there were elected leaders who adhered to a set of bylaws that the workers themselves produced, voted on, and implemented.

As a consultant hired by the Lusty workers, Farrell held a subsumed class position and was paid to try to save the theater. Typically, WSDEs hire workers who ensure their conditions of existence. Farrell, however, believed that his job was to dismantle the WSDE structure, which clearly would have destroyed their conditions of existence. There is a serious and obvious contradiction between Farrell's employment by the Lusty and the workers' desire to remain a collective/WSDE. I am not suggesting that Farrell was *the* essential agent in the Lusty's demise; however, had a New Marxian Class Analysis been available at the time, the outcome might have been different.

Forbes, the landlord, also held a subsumed class position. He had no association with the enterprise, except to collect (and raise) the rent. He did this drastically, which had a significant role in closing the Lusty. While he may not have had a direct interest in the theater, Forbes bought not only the Lusty property in 1998, but also an entire parcel of land that includes Larry Flint's

Hustler Club (Roberts, 2013). Furthermore as reporter Chris Roberts wrote in *SF Weekly*, "it's official: when it comes to adult entertainment, San Francisco is a monopoly town—and not a local one at that" (ibid.).[10]

All of the San Francisco clubs are LLCs, or Limited Liability Companies. LLCs, which came into being in the 1990s, were not intended to be long-term enterprises, but that is what they have become. As I have written elsewhere, LLCs have the protections from personal liabilities that corporations have, but with tax obligations limited to those of a partnership, and this explains why we are seeing more and more of them (Mulder, 2009). The San Francisco strip clubs are owned by BSC Management, Déjà Vu Entertainment and 250 Columbus Avenue, all of which have the same Seattle, Washington, post office box as their address (Roberts, 2013; Swan 2013). Forbes, then, was not just a landlord, but in direct competition with the Lusty Lady, and for this reason had a considerable incentive to evict them. Moreover, as Swan states, because Forbes is not a local businessperson, he is less likely to be concerned "with the cultural history of the neighborhood" than he is with profits (2013). In NMCA terms, Forbes and his associates received subsumed class payments as landlords, but had no intention of remaining so—unlike most landlords, who prefer long-term tenants (except where there are rent controls). The Lusty collective made subsumed class payments to an agent who wanted it to fail.

As in the LSO case, the Lusty also had a "support staff" that secured their conditions of existence as a worker cooperative. However, the members of the Lusty staff were included as members of the cooperative, and this means that the enterprise did not have a truly WSDE class structure within NMCA framework. To be a "perfect" example of a WSDE, the surplus producers must be the first recipients of the surplus. As required by the California Consumer Cooperative Law, members of the Lusty's support staff were also among the first recipients of the surplus produced by the dancers. They "enjoyed" all the rights, privileges, costs, and voice that the productive performers had. While the support staff received subsumed class payments from the surplus for their work as janitors, cashiers, bouncers, and the like, they also occupied the fundamental class position of the surplus's direct recipients—problematic within NMCA in a *purely* WSDE. Because these non-surplus-producing workers have a voice in the production process, from the NMCA perspective, the Lusty's support staff were exploiters.

In an email exchange on January 27, 2015, I asked Richard Wolff (one of the NMCA developers) how he and the late Steve Resnick addressed this very issue, given that democratic principles would dictate that all workers in a firm should have the same voting power—that is, one vote per worker. Wolff responded:

> If anyone other than productive laborers receives/appropriates the surplus, those others are exploiters. What a WSDE [communist class structure] or true workers cooperative must do, if it is to avoid exploitation and all the conflicts and tensions thereby entailed, is to constitute two executive bodies: (1) one body to appropriate and distribute the surplus—a body composed exclusively of the productive laborers, and (2) another body composed of both productive and unproductive laborers who decide collectively and democratically what portions of the surplus to distribute to whom and for what. The second body has the power to make all those decisions about production and distribution of the surplus. The first body actually produces and appropriates and does the distribution.[11]

The Lusty Lady came very close, but it did not quite manage to meet this criterion. Indeed, in some of the conversations/interviews I had with dancers and support staff, both groups reported tensions—they simply had different issues and responsibilities. Given the stress related to the imminent closing, this added to the already tense situation.

## Conclusion

The Lusty Lady will always be remembered as the little theater that could—it could organize itself into a union, buy out the capitalist employers, and operate and manage a self-governed enterprise, almost a true WSDE, for a decade. However, because of the circumstances, particularly with the exorbitant monthly rent, the Lusty workers had no alternative than to shutter its doors. Thus, the question arises: What could have been done to save this operation? The answers are multifaceted and overdetermined by a variety of processes, political, economic, and cultural.

When the Lusty workers attempted to unionize in 1996, they were met with resistance from various unions, even the SEIU. According to attorney Holly J. Wilmet:

> The Lusty Lady dancers, who sought out Service Employees International Union (SEIU), local 790 representation, initially encountered resistance from that union; but local 790 had an informal affiliation with the Exotic Dancers' Alliance, a San Francisco-based advocacy group, and with their assistance, persuaded local 790 to represent them. (1998, 467, n. 8)

Wilmet believed that there were moral as well as illegal economic reasons for unions to shy away from representing this group of workers. She attributed it to "the controversial and sexual nature of these professions, the industry's reputed ties to organized crime, fear of public backlash," and even to the National Labor Relations Act that prohibits workers from unionizing if they have supervisory duties or are "independent contractors" (ibid., 468).

Until relatively recently, many sex workers were deemed independent contractors and even paid fees so they could work. While this was never the case at the Lusty—they were always considered employees—it is the case with many of the other clubs across the country. However, in November 2014, strippers and sex workers won a federal court case making them employees instead of independent contractors. This ruling means that dancers can now file for unemployment insurance and receive Social Security benefits and the many other benefits that come with being ruled as an employee (Gregorian, 2014).[12] As independent contractors, dancers actually had to pay to be exploited; now they are earning wages, but continue to be exploited.

Wilmet also believes that once sex-workers know their rights and are legitimized, they will be prime targets for union organizing drives. She states:

By denying its existence and legitimacy, a hypocritical society pushes the industry underground and out of sight, whereby illegal and exploitative practices such as those described herein, are allowed and even encouraged to flourish unabated and unchecked. Perhaps a better solution is one where all factions of the adult entertainment industry are recognized, tolerated, legitimized, legalized, and regulated when necessary, either by state or local government—as on Nevada's brothels. In this way, those working in the industry can be assured of safe and non-exploitative working conditions, acceptable wages, access to necessary medical and social services, and legislative protection. Society would, in return, benefit from a decreased risk of transmittable social diseases, less burden on the welfare system and increased tax revenues. (Wilmet 1998, 472)

Given the recent news that union density in the private sector is still decreasing and is currently under 10 percent, one would think these organizations would pursue organizing these workers *en masse*. She states:

The unionization of adult entertainers is already in progress and promises to continue with ever-increasing speed as greater numbers of dancers, informed of their legal rights and empowered by their brethren's success, gather the knowledge and courage to stand up for their legal and civil rights. The unionization of exotic dancers promises to be like no other in modern history. Not only will it be a new chapter in the history of the labor movement, but it promises to be the birth of a new breed of feminism: a movement where beauty is a sword, not a shield; and where women bare their bras, not burn them. (ibid., 473)

If we did not think about doing this kind of work as anti-feminist or amoral, and thought of these people as workers, perhaps the Lusty would have survived. There seems to be no concerted effort by the authorities to look into the monopolization of the industry, simply because of the nature of the work.

In view of the fact that the Lusty Lady was a non-profit enterprise operated by its workers, the San Francisco legislature could have instituted rent control laws. As discussed above, the rent was simply not within the means of the Lusty workers. The workers even took to the streets to ask for donations just to make payroll.

And where was the SEIU? The SEIU could have lobbied the local authorities for rent controls, but I have not seen any evidence of that. Indeed, Delinqua told me that the Lusty workers felt like the "red-headed stepchild" and were basically ignored by the union.

One final note: in the United States, the only federal labor law is the National Labor Relations Act,[13] which excludes supervisors from union membership. The NLRA does not support workers who are self-governed and self-managed. For this reason, unions may be reluctant to work with this type of organization because they simply do not know how to deal with this structure. The information I gathered in my talks with some of the Lusty workers suggests that the union did very little to assist these workers in saving their jobs. Yet unions can and should use their resources to help workers who want to remain self-governed.[14] Union officials, however, seem to perpetuate the "us versus them" mindset; although they may attempt to resist the encroachment of capitalism, they do nothing to help change the economic system. As Marx said:

> Trades Unions work well as centres of resistance against the encroachments of capital. They fail partially from an injudicious use of their power. They fail generally from limiting themselves to a guerrilla war against the existing system, instead of simultaneously tying to change it, instead of using their organized forces as a lever for the final emancipation of the working class, that is to say, the ultimate abolition of the wages system. (Marx, 1997, 62)

The Lusty workers, who for a decade did manage to transcend capitalism through cooperative practice, richly deserve our admiration and respect.

The dancers at the Lusty Lady were truly groundbreaking feminists who had chosen to work in the adult-entertainment industry. But when they believed they were being taken advantage of, they organized themselves into a union. Typically, unions send representatives to worksites to organize the workers, yet the Lusty Lady workers had a difficult time finding an existing trade union that would represent their interests, even at a time when union density is declining rapidly. It was finally the SEIU that came to their assistance. Even though the Lusty Lady has now closed, what these workers did was truly remarkable: their story began when they were abused and exploited workers and concluded with their creation of a self-governing cooperative that lasted for more than a decade.

The workers I met and spoke with were somewhat anxious about their future after the Lusty closed, but they are strong, and they are survivors. The Lusty Lady workers will be memorialized for many years. Had it not been for the adverse circumstances in the political, economic, and cultural environment in which they toiled, they probably would still be in business. If limits had been set on rent increases, for example, the Lusties might be working today. But when a small enterprise like the Lusty must confront a huge monopoly like Déjà Vu, it can have very little chance of surviving. The one benefit to the Lusty workers was that they could apply for unemployment insurance, having established that they were not independent contractors. Not much of a prize, admittedly, but it is at least something to keep them afloat. I remain in contact with several of the workers, and I know that while they are disheartened, they are admirably resilient—as must be obvious from their conduct throughout their struggles.

# CHAPTER 4

# New Era Windows Cooperative: From a Sit-Down Strike to a Worker Cooperative

"We are here and not going anywhere."[1]

"We win what we fight for."[2]

## Introduction

When I began this book project and chose the New Era workers as a case study, my intent was to emphasize how the United Electrical Radio and Machine Workers of America (UE) missed a perfect opportunity to facilitate a revolution in the class structure of this enterprise. I found it incomprehensible that a different work structure was apparently not even considered. It seemed to me that the only answer the UE had was to help find another capitalist to own and run the firm. Though they missed their first opportunity, however, the workers changed their strategy when the second capitalist employer opted to close the plant. In 2013, New Era Windows Cooperative, a democratic worker cooperative, was open for business, but only after moving to a smaller location with some very dedicated, hardworking people. Indeed, the workers initiated a class revolution and opted for the egalitarian Worker Self-Directed Enterprise (WSDE) instead of the autocratic capitalist class structure to which they were accustomed.

## Background

In 1996, the city of Chicago gave Republic Windows and Doors a $10 million grant to move the business to a new location on the city's Goose Island, an industrial space where other factories and plants are located (Lydersen, 2009, 25). The new facility was spacious, sterile, and state of the art, with the latest in machinery, comfortable cafeterias and break rooms, even a gym (ibid). In its heyday, Republic employed approximately 500 workers, but that number dwindled to about 250 by 2008.

That year, even after receiving the taxpayers' $10 million grant, Republic decided to move their operations to Iowa and other locations without informing the workers; many of them had become suspicious, however, having noticed that inventory and machines were disappearing. The president of the UE Local 1110, Armando Robles, staked out the factory in his car for a couple of evenings and saw the machinery being taken away in U-Haul trucks. This was naturally of a cause of great concern for him and his colleagues, especially when they discovered that Republic was delivering the machinery to a non-union facility in Iowa. It was a shockingly sneaky process, with trucks coming in and being loaded with both office furniture and machinery in the middle of the night.

The workers were right to be suspicious. Republic abruptly informed them that the Chicago factory would close in three days (ibid., 58). The workers were frightened but also outraged (Ricky Maclin, interview with author, July 22, 2013), and, rather than retreating, these brave men and women staged an old-fashioned "sit-down strike," something we have not seen in the United States since the 1930s. These workers, about 300 strong at this point, united and some 65 of them simply refused for six days to leave the factory. They were committed to their work and realized that, without them, the factory would produce nothing.

The media deemed this action extremely radical, and it made national and even international news, being covered in *Le Monde* and *Al-Jazeera*, among other news outlets (Lydersen, 2009, 73). It also prompted journalist Kari Lydersen to write her book *Revolt on Goose Island*, which recounts their story up until 2008. The news of the sit-down strike went "viral," thereby garnering support from other unions, activists, government officials, religious leaders, and community members. People understood the workers' outrage—after all, it was almost Christmas and the Republic workers, now unemployed, had been denied severance and back vacation pay, benefits, and the requisite legal notice as stated in the Worker Adjustment and Retraining Notification (WARN) Act of 1988.[3]

While most of the workers' complaints were justified, the most serious consequence of the factory closure was their loss of severance and back pay; the company informed them that the Bank of America had refused their traditional line of credit to Republic for the payment of wages. Many people are unaware that corporations, even small businesses, have a "line of credit" that they use to pay employees' wages. Many incorrectly assume that businesses have adequate funds to meet payroll before hiring the workers, but, in fact, the former practice is quite common. New firms often have difficulty establishing a line of credit, and this is yet another barrier for new collectives/cooperatives and WSDEs. A line of credit is needed for corporations to ensure their conditions of existence for resource payments. What particularly angered the workers was that the Bank of America had just been given a bailout of $25 billion from the federal government through the Troubled Asset Relief Program (TARP), along with an "undisclosed share of some $4 trillion the Federal Reserve Board [had] handed out directly to major financial concerns" (Eley, 2008). After an embarrassing protest outside the Bank of America offices in central Chicago, Republic agreed to pay each worker $6000 and the sit-down strike ended after six days with the workers claiming victory.

The $6000 victory was bittersweet, in that the workers remained unemployed. A few months later, however, a new owner purchased the company for $1.45 million, taking advantage of the American Recovery and Reinvestment Act (ARRA). The company was now owned by Serious Materials, a "green" California capitalist enterprise that makes not only windows, but also energy-efficient drywall. Although Serious had agreed to many of the UE demands (Lydersen, 2009, 1),[4] the company ultimately hired back only about 72 workers[5] and within two years closed its doors, blaming the collapse of the housing market (St. John, 2012). The workers for their part blamed the Serious management and its unworkable business plan, which involved the windows factory in a merely tertiary role. The company had to make drastic reductions its operations and was finally forced to close the factory.[6] The workers first staged another sit-in but then decided to purchase the company themselves and form a democratic/cooperative work environment. Robles, the local union president, had mentioned the possibility of such a reorganization before Serious bought the company, when he returned from the 2006 "World Social Forum" in Caracas, Venezuela. The Forum enabled Robles the opportunity to speak with workers from around the world and it became clear to him in the course of these conversations that the bosses needed the workers, but that the reverse was not necessarily true (Robles, interview with author, July 23, 2013). But according to Ricky Maclin (who is vice president of the new company), it was only in 2012 that he and the other workers were ready to embark on the life-altering endeavor of forming their own company.

## A New Era for Chicago Window Workers

Forming a collective in a predominantly capitalist environment is anything but easy. Indeed, when I interviewed the workers, they all commented on the difficulties they were enduring, albeit willingly. The most daunting issue they faced was that Serious refused to sell the factory's equipment and machinery to the workers. According to the workers, Serious had bought the equipment two years earlier at rock-bottom prices, but they refused the offer from this group of workers to purchase it from them. The California-based CEO did not realize with whom he was dealing. The UE, Occupy Chicago, and other groups organized and contacted the media, including *Democracy Now*, and filmed their own documentary, *The Take*. They also petitioned the community and received over three thousand signatures within one day. Serious backed down and, although coerced, they did eventually agree to sell the machinery to these workers. With the help of The Working World and its president, Brendan Martin, they were able to borrow enough money from The Working World to purchase the machinery with a low-interest line of credit of $645,000 in May 2012; $450,000 was spent for raw materials and equipment, and the remaining $195,000 was to be distributed as needed.[7] Each cooperative member was also required to pay $1000 for their share of the company, an amount that may seem small but was in fact difficult for many of the workers to raise. One member even borrowed the money from his nephew.

The workers, now only 17 of them, including The Working World's Brendan Martin, purchased the necessary machinery and moved it to a new, much smaller location on the southwest side of Chicago. According to Robles, the new location had previously been a warehouse, and thus there was much to be done to transform it into a window factory. The workers did everything themselves: they rented moving vans, installed electricity and plumbing, and even did all the cleaning. In addition to acquiring these skills, every cooperative owner is learning how to do every job in the factory, from accounting to producing the windows.

It took approximately one year to move and begin operations, at which time the workers did not pay themselves a salary. I asked each of them during my two-day visit to the factory in July 2013 how they were surviving financially, and while the answers varied, it was obvious that they were all enduring many hardships. While looking for jobs to tide them over, some of them received unemployment compensation. Those who did qualify for unemployment benefits received funding from The Working World (ibid.). Though the financial distress of these workers was apparent, they were all optimistic about the future. According to Alejandra Cancino in a November 2013 article in the *Chicago Tribune*, the workers finally began drawing a salary, but it was less than the state's $8.25 minimum wage (2013).

I think it is important to note that with the exception of Martin, the cooperative's members are either African American or Latino. These workers' efforts and dedication are clear evidence that our society's widespread negative stereotypes and discriminatory beliefs about these groups are blatantly false. During my two days in the New Era factory, I witnessed something truly remarkable, a group of workers who collaborated and worked for a common goal, held meetings, attempted to get sales, and did whatever needed to be done. I was, however, surprised by the time clock on the wall. Each worker punched in and out, which seemed to me inappropriate in a collaborative atmosphere. However, when I asked Robles about this, he told me that they had agreed as a collective to count their worked hours so that, when they were finally able to pay themselves, there would be no discrepancies. (While I did not see one, I later learned that the workers at the Lusty Lady also used a time clock.) Moreover, in contrast to a typical capitalist work environment, workers were free to take time off for a doctor's appointment or for some other personal reason.

## The Working World

The workers at both the Lusty Lady and New Era told me that the most difficult part of forming and operating a cooperative or a democratically organized firm is financing. This is where The Working World came to the rescue of the workers in Chicago. According to its website, The Working World resembles venture capitalists in that the organization loans money, which they expect to be repaid with interest, to enterprises with a "radical social mission." Unlike venture capitalists, however, The Working World is a non-profit enterprise; its primary focus is to assist workers in a variety of communities to purchase and operate their own firms. Currently, they have ventures in Argentina, Nicaragua, and now the United States. They claim in their website to:

> support worker cooperatives using a finance model that puts money at the service of people, not the other way around. We help design, fund, and carry out productive projects, only requiring that cooperatives pay us back with the revenues the investments generate. As active partners, we are more motivated to ensure that these projects are successful, or in other words, that finance is only used as a tool to create real, lasting wealth for those that it serves. Upon return, all investment money is reintegrated

to our locally-based revolving loan fund to be overseen by the cooperatives and the community it serves.[8]

According to Robles and Maclin, this is not just a claim but a reality. New Era would have never even opened its doors had it not been for the financing from The Working World and the dedicated people, particularly Martin who administer it.

The Working World does not simply loan these democratic firms money, but also provides valuable resources to fledgling businesses: assistance in creating a business plan, conducting negotiations, and acquiring other vital skills needed to run the business. Often, The Working World even provides the companies with interns and office help, given the workers' unfamiliarity with various business practices. One requirement is that the firms be organized democratically, with one vote per worker and with leaders who are elected by the membership. At New Era, Robles is the current president and Maclin is the vice president, and the two also serve as *elected* managers. The workers are encouraged to have weekly meetings, and Maclin said that New Era does this, except during their busiest seasons, when they have to get the product completed on time. Sometimes, the New Era meetings are lengthy, but all of the workers hold them in high regard.

As we have seen, during the company's first year, when they built and moved into the new facility, the New Era workers rarely received any wages. Martin and his team at The Working World gave much encouragement and other non-financial support, however, and, according to most of the workers, this alone was enough to maintain their commitment to this factory and their work. Times have been rough—but the workers remain optimistic about their prospects and expect to secure three rather large orders in the near future (Maclin, phone interview with author, February 16, 2015). When I asked Maclin whether he missed having a supervisor and whether all this work was worth it, he laughed and said that he is "eternally grateful" for the way things are evolving.

During some of the more difficult times, The Working World did the opposite of what a bank or credit union would do when firms cannot repay their loans. Rather than closing New Era down and demanding repayment, The Working World loaned additional funds to New Era to get the company through the tough times. The recent hiring of an experienced salesman, who receives both a salary and a commission, has made the workers more optimistic than ever. One can only hope that their optimism is justified.[9]

## The United Electrical Radio and Machine Workers of America (UE)

The UE is an independent union that does not belong to any umbrella organization such as the AFL-CIO or Change to Win. I have always considered it quite progressive, not only in the political arena, but also in its internal operations; unlike other trade unions, the UE is very democratic. For this reason, I was surprised that the UE did not help the workers form their own enterprise when Republic closed. In my previous book, *Unions and Class Transformation: The Case of the Broadway Musicians* (Mulder, 2009), I detailed how unions could and should assist workers who choose to become "bossless." Although the UE initially failed to do this, the union did arrange protests and leafleting, and contacted and organized other labor unions and activists, and it was also instrumental in getting the workers their severance package of $6000.

I found the workers' attitude toward their union much different than what I usually encounter. These workers were losing their jobs, some after working decades for the same employer, but they did *not* blame the union for their woes—they knew precisely who shut down Republic and it was not the UE. Their spirit, militancy, solidarity, and dedication to the UE were not only astounding, but also quite refreshing. Having been both a paid employee and an active union representative for more than thirty years, I know that workers' animosity toward their union, particularly when a plant closes, is the typical. These workers were different. "The members run this union" is a quote from the top of the UE homepage; it anything but your typical top-down union structure.[10]

As was the case with the Lusty Lady workers, every worker in the plant is a union member, even though the firm is now a cooperative. Indeed, the New Era workers are, at the time of this writing, in the process of negotiating and working out the terms of a collective-bargaining agreement to be ratified soon. Interestingly enough, the collective-bargaining agreement that is being negotiated by Robles and officials at the UE is very similar to the bylaws the workers have in place. Negotiations have a very different outcome when it is not an "us versus them" situation. Indeed, as at the Lusty, so also here: "us are them."

The UE does not simply stay out of the workers' way; it supports and promotes non-exploitative, sustainable democratic economic development. The union's webpage proudly proclaims the advantages of a non-exploitative arrangement. It states:

> Consumer and worker-owned-and-operated cooperatives are a natural place for UE members to reside and are an important sector in our union's future. There is a growing interest within our country in how the working class can begin to develop and support the creation of more democratic and sustainable business models, where the motivation for those involved in the enterprise is not greed and profit but building environmentally sustainable union jobs whose product or work provide value to our communities through good pay, benefits, and healthy and safe work environments. For UE, there is no better way to be productive than as a rank-and-file democratic trade union or a worker-owned enterprise. UE co-ops share our union's proud history and fighting spirit. They also benefit from our reputation as a union with vision, integrity, and commitment that works in a principled way with other organizations in building a better world. [11]

While the UE may give only non-financial support to New Era, it does encourage its members to pool their resources and form community and environmentally friendly cooperatives. However, moreover while the UE has not provided financing, the workers are not required to pay union dues while they are building their enterprise and struggling to get it off the ground. When I spoke with Maclin recently, however, he said that he is looking forward to the time when he can pay his dues again; in fact, he said that "it's the only right thing to do." It is important to point out that by federal law, the only legal source of income for unions is money that is received as dues payments. Thus, not collecting dues but continuing to assist the cooperative is extremely generous on the part of the UE—something other unions might not do.

One final thought on the UE and unions in general: many other unions are so entrenched in the management/labor arrangement that, when mention is made of infringing on a management's "rights" or prerogatives, the comment is met with hostility. I have witnessed this firsthand a number of times. For the future of the labor movement and for workers in general, worker advocates need to follow the example of The Working World and the UE in supporting democratic business models. Capital and technological improvements, particularly in communications, are making it to easy for firms to move their operations overseas or to southern states where the union membership rates are lower than in the North, and there are many states that have "right-to-work" laws that make unions basically moot. We must remember that the unionization of a collective does not violate the National Labor Relations Act, which prohibits supervisors from being organized. Since there are no supervisors, there can be no violation, and the workers at New Era Windows Cooperative have chosen to remain members of the UE.

### NMCA and New Era

The New Era Cooperative, if not the epitome of a WSDE using the NMCA methodology, is very close to it. Each of the current 19 owner-workers takes turns doing the various work needed to produce their windows, which they claim are less expensive and of better quality than Pella and Anderson replacement windows. Because there is no board of directors or CEO or CFO or other high-paid employees, the workers believe they can maintain their low prices. As of my visit in the summer of 2013, they had some orders for their products, but, of course, they were working very hard to find more. Most of their customers at that time were union members and progressive activists in the Chicago area, but the New Era workers were doing what they could with limited funding to spread their net. Maclin, whose position at the time was in sales, was on the phone taking orders and selling their products practically non-stop. They are doing their best not to suffer the same fate as the Lusty Lady.

When I asked Robles how they had decided which 17 workers would be part of the cooperative—there had been over 70 workers when Serious owned the company, and almost 300 had worked for Republic Windows and Doors—he was very quick to answer, "[W]e chose people who would cooperate with each other." Cooperation was their primary objective, and less important than expertise, which I found fascinating. Workers had to agree to train, teach, and learn all the aspects of making windows, in addition to the other trades they needed to learn in order to get the factory going.

Analyzing the New Era Cooperative is a relatively straightforward process. All the cooperative members occupy not only the fundamental class position as producers of surplus when they are making the windows, but also hold the fundamental class position of surplus appropriators. These same workers occupy the subsumed class positions as surplus distributors, although at the time of my visit there was no surplus being produced—simply because they were yet to produce and therefore sell the windows to realize any surplus. The assumption was that in due course there will be surplus, from which they will have to make distributions in order to secure their conditions of existence as a WSDE.

They have now been in production since New Era opened on May 9, 2013. It is important to note, however, the stresses caused by required payments for rent, taxes, raw materials, wages for "specialists," and capital stock, payments in excess of revenues from sales, met only by using the initial line of credit and the cooperative membership fee. Fortunately for the New Era workers, other subsumed class payments (repayment of the original loan and a supplementary one from The Working World, and union dues) have been, for now, suspended. However, since New Era workers are currently not realizing sufficient gross revenue to cover even the remaining portion of costs, their conditions of existence as a WSDE are being compromised, forcing them to hire a professional salesman to focus on sales to wholesalers.[12] The workers are performing useful labor, using machinery to transform raw materials, thus adding value to the windows produced, and yet they are unable to realize revenue sufficient to pay themselves the minimum wage, let alone yield a surplus over and above that. The value added by their labors, necessary as well as surplus labor, is captured elsewhere (by customers or by input and credit providers), due to their inability to sell at a price sufficient even to cover the collective's out-of-pocket costs.[13]

A typical capitalist firm in similar circumstances would probably have closed by now. The difference here is that the workers have a vision and a stake in its fulfillment. They admit that they are sometimes apprehensive, yet they know it is up to them to make the decision to remain in production or close. The decision is not in someone else's hands. Finally, as with any collective, communication is vital: the workers continue to meet once a week for meetings to discuss issues and distributions. Are there disagreements? Of course. But the members of the collective seem to be working them out.

## Conclusion

At the time of this writing, New Era remains open and is gaining sales. The cooperative members were still earning a bit less than minimum wage, and one of the original members has accepted a more lucrative position and left the company; however, during this "slow season" according to Maclin, they are once again forgoing any self-payments. The cooperative has hired three workers, a casement-window expert, a maintenance person, and a professional salesman. According to Maclin, these workers have not yet become cooperative members; it is part of New Era's primary philosophy that new workers be compatible with the rest of the membership, and so there is a one-year probation period written into their bylaws. After the year is over, the current members will vote on whether to invite the new workers to join the collective. The one-year probation time might seem a bit long, but the members view the collective like a "marriage": once a worker has become a member, it is more difficult to separate. One could argue that the cooperative members are capitalists as long as there are workers who are not part of the collective and are receiving a salary, but I see it as an investment by these non-member workers into their own labor power, just as if they were attending college or trade school. In a capitalist enterprise, there is no promise that workers will ever have any control over the surplus; this is the difference between New Era's structure and an exploitative structure (capitalism, for example). During the probationary year, new workers are learning not only about being part of the collective, but like every collective member are also being taught new skills in other aspects of the business. Recall that each member is required to know how to do the jobs of all their colleagues, from accounting to working on the production line. The probationary members are learning this in their first year.

According to Maclin, business is improving, even though they are currently in their "slow season." He was proud to announce that they are now producing casement windows as well as those originally in production, and they have hired a new worker who has that expertise. The members at this time (March 2015) are not receiving wages, but they are reaping other rewards, such as the promise of higher wages in the future and not having to worry about being fired without cause. Thus, even though their revenues doubled in the past year according to The Working World's newsletter, the surplus that the New Era workers are currently producing is not sufficient to sustain the enterprise. When the members are drawing salaries, they are much lower than the average wage, and lower than their wages when they worked for Republic or Serious.

While struggling to stay afloat, New Era nevertheless made the collective decision to hire a professional sales person so that their surplus can be realized. This person, according to The Working World's 2014 newsletter, is "one of the more famous salesmen in the Chicago Area" (Martin, 2014). They also collectively added two more jobs that they believe should increase their surplus, a "veteran line worker, and a master mechanic" (ibid.). The cooperative members decided to expand the types of windows they were producing and increased its investment into capital stock by buying out the bankrupt Armaclad Windows, ironically owned by

Republic Windows. "The factory closure left a gap in the market that New Era has moved into, capturing new accounts valued at hundreds of thousands of dollars in annual revenue" (ibid.). The purchase of this factory required an expert in casement windows; hence the collective's decision to hire a "master mechanic."

The cooperative member who resigned during the first year was replaced with a "veteran line worker," and, with the hiring of the salesman and master mechanic, the number of workers has increased to 21. The New Era Cooperative has also "constructed a state-of-the-art paint facility," and, because the members did the work themselves, they saved a "tremendous" amount of money. In fact, their entire total investment of capital was less than 10 percent of their nearest competitor. Saving much-needed revenues has enabled New Era to be sustainable in a "hyper-competitive" market (ibid). Robles spent three weeks learning the skills necessary for painting the windows—which Maclin said are more valuable once painted—and now Robles is considered the "master painter" and is training others to do the job.

Though the members were quite nervous and had their doubts about New Era's success, they have proven that a small group of workers can run, maintain, and, in the future, profit from their investments, not only in capital, but in labor power as well. "New Era is nothing short of a miracle" (ibid.). In capitalist firms, capital controls labor. New Era has shown that labor can control capital.

## Epilogue

As the New Era workers continue to struggle, they remain optimistic about their future. In winter 2014–2015, the workers (not including the non-members) again decided not to draw a salary. But, given the hope of new orders from a few big contractors, they think this will be only temporary. New Era also no longer sells directly to consumers; instead, they sell to installers, contractors, and wholesalers. This type of arrangement is typical in most enterprises in the United States; rarely do consumers buy directly from warehouses.[14]

When I visited the plant in July 2012, I spoke to every worker, including those who do not speak English. Since my Spanish is limited to the very basics, I interviewed some workers with the help of one of the other workers, who acted as my interpreters. Every worker was a bit hesitant to talk to me at first but, for whatever reasons, opened up in the end. They all believed firmly in New Era's success, but all of them were facing extreme hardships—not earning a salary, having no health or dental benefits, and working many hours doing things that were not necessarily their specialties. They also made it clear to me that they were not only committed to the success of New Era, but also to the friendships they had formed with their co-workers, with whom they had little in common except for their work. They all ate lunch together, brought in food for each other—it was like a traditional family Sunday dinner. I was surprised and touched by this. During my interview with Maclin on February 16, 2015, I asked about the communication problem with English versus Spanish and whether they have found a way to solve it. Maclin said that the workers are learning to communicate better but that there was more to be done. He thought it might be beneficial to offer both Spanish and English lessons for all the workers.

We also spoke about health benefits and the political situation in Illinois. Maclin said that most of the workers had some insurance thanks to President Obama's Affordable Care Act. (We both had a laugh when I referred to it as Obamacare, and Maclin was quick to respond that he doesn't like what has happened to the term Obamacare and refuses to use it. He is grateful that he can get health insurance now thanks to this act.) Maclin also spoke about the new Republican governor of Illinois, Bruce Rauner. Maclin informed me that Rauner, like other Republican governors, was trying to implement a right-to-work law, thus making unionization passé.[15] Maclin also said, however, that Rauner had visited their plant and was impressed by their entrepreneurial endeavors; the Governor had indicated that the state might be able to offer some assistance, but Maclin was not optimistic about such a possibility. Nevertheless, he was pleased that this Republican governor, unlike his Democrat predecessor, had at least taken notice of their enterprise and the difficulties it was facing. I asked whether New Era received any state or city subsidies and learned that to date they have not. Maclin also mentioned a visit from Vice President Biden when Serious took over the plant. Biden was enthusiastic about the new ownership and was confident that it would be good for the city and the workers. Maclin said that he has heard nothing from Vice President Biden or President Obama's office since that time. He commented that he was disappointed in President Obama but not really surprised. Maclin and I chatted about how the President and his office have made no concerted effort to improve working conditions for the masses or to challenge capitalist exploitation. We even laughed about the erroneous notion that the President is a socialist. It seems to us that he is simply reinforcing the status quo.

We also discussed the question of whether New Era will remain unionized, even though the company has no managers, board of directors, or the like. When I asked whether he thought the union would be superfluous, he informed me that the workers had every intention of staying with the UE; indeed, Maclin said that it is important to have a collective-bargaining agreement to protect "him from himself." He would not want to work so much that his health would suffer. While the UE does not provide any financial support, it does provide solidarity and information that the New Era workers need and appreciate and moreover acts as a mediator between the workers if a problem should arise. Maclin put it this way: "It's a win/win situation."

According to Maclin, the members of the New Era collective have every expectation that the new workers and the salesman will become members soon, given that their one-year probation period is about to expire. When I asked him about the possibility that they might not want to join, he was astonished, saying, "Who wouldn't want to own their own business?" We agreed that that is in fact the "American Dream." When Republic closed the plant, Maclin explained, they had not yet developed the "owner mentality." But when Serious announced its plans to close, the workers were "pushed into a corner" and then really battled back.

After two years of working for Serious, Maclin said, "they were ready." Furthermore, as Brendan Martin states: "New Era has proven their vision: a group of workers can build a manufacturer as good as any and compete for the future of our economy" (Martin, 2014, 3).

CHAPTER 5

# A Worker Self-Directed Enterprise in State Capitalist Cuba! The Case of Organopónico Vivero Alamar

## Introduction

In June 2012, I had the pleasure of visiting Cuba for research and a conference—long before the dramatic turn of events with the United States that included the relaxation of the embargo that had been in place since the early 1960s and that was tightened in 1992. The trip was organized by scholars and activists who, like me, wanted to learn about alternatives to the economic and social structures that are currently prevalent in the United States. This was one of the most fascinating trips of my life; the culture, the politics, the economy, and even the environment were quite unfamiliar to a US scholar. Many of the stories about Cuba that I had heard all my life (I was born in 1959) turned out to be simply untrue—the Cuban people were happy, healthy, and culturally astute, and, in the years since the collapse of the USSR in the early 1990s, they have been making energetic efforts to improve their living and working situations.[1]

During my visit in June, the weather was sweltering, and, unfortunately, amenities that we take for granted in the United States—air conditioning, for example—were simply not available in many places. As expected, we saw many of the 1950s American-made cars that are celebrated in the States. However, because of the embargo and the extreme shortage of parts, most of these cars have been rebuilt and now have diesel engines and emit black soot through their exhaust pipes, making breathing a bit difficult. Thanks to the heat and the soot from the cars, the comfort level left much to be desired. There was also only a limited and very slow connection to the Internet, and one had the feeling that Cuba was, and had long been, isolated from the rest of the world. But happily, I found myself in the midst of a nevertheless very inventive and creative group of people. When I asked one gentleman how they kept the old cars running for so long, he told me that it was done with "rubber bands and paper clips"; seeing my shocked expression, he then reminded me that "necessity is the mother of invention." And indeed, because of the US embargo, the Cuban population has needed many things—but somehow they have managed.

The 1950s cars are typically not in use by individuals, but rather are used as taxis, which transport as many people as they can fit into them. Also used for taxis are ancient cars imported from the former Soviet Union, which barely run and for which spare parts are no longer available. But in spite of these inconveniences, Cuba has wonderful cultural events, artists, frequent and accessible mass transportation, and the Cuban people are working diligently to improve their infrastructure. I had the opportunity to speak to some local residents, and they made it very clear that they could not get anything that contained even a small part that was made in the United States. (I was amazed one day, though, to see a brand-new Dodge Charger parked on a street—how it got there remains a mystery.) This was not because Cuba prohibited imports, but because the United States prohibited exports. By the time this book is published, the relaxation or lifting of the embargo should be complete, and imports and exports will be flowing more freely.

Cuba has witnessed so many political, social, and economic changes (and, no doubt, also environmental ones) that I cannot hope to include in this chapter an analysis of all their effects on the Cuban people and society. The scope of such an analysis would be far too broad for this book. Instead, this chapter will isolate, and to some extent encapsulate, one particular urban farm in Havana, the nation's capital. This remarkable enterprise, *Organopónico Vivero Alamar*, has flourished in the wake of the changes and socioeconomic experiments forced upon Cuba after the fall of the USSR.

## The Farm: Organopónico Vivero Alamar

Organopónico Vivero Alamar is the urban organic farm (from this point forward, I will simply refer to it as "the Farm") that I visited during my trip. It is a fascinating example of a small farm, one of the many that were created when the state-run farms within this centrally planned Communist country were divided. In this context, the word "Communist" does not refer to collective appropriation of the surplus by the workers. Rather, it refers instead to the more widely known definition of a dictatorial form of government and an economy that is owned, operated, and managed by the state, in this case by Cuba. In fact, I would argue that, prior to the post-1992 experiments, Cuba was not communist at all, but rather a state-run capitalist society (Mulder, 2015; Resnick and Wolff, 2002). The farm to be investigated here represents one of the successful Cuban socioeconomic experiments, and, although I cannot include all possible variables in my discussion, a New Marxian Class Analysis will reveal some very interesting features of its organizational structure.

The Farm was founded in 1987 and consists of 29 acres of land. It is one of 154 farms that are privately run or operated with state involvement, but that made changes in their organizational structure after the fall of the USSR. Those who work on the Farm are proud to call it a worker cooperative, and they have educational sessions and tours right on the property. Moreover, its vision and mission statement make it clear that it is a worker cooperative and shall remain that way. It states:

> Organopónico Vivero Alamar is to be a cooperative farm, focusing on agricultural production and services. Dedicated to professionalism, honesty, immediacy, discipline, hospitality and the shared values of commitment to the country and to the individual, Vivero Alamar strives to be a national and global leader in sustainable agriculture.
>
> Organopónico Vivero Alamar contributes to the needs of people, offering a wide range of vegetables, ornamental and medicinal

plants, and other food products. Vivero Alamar also provides community services, applies innovations in science and technology to the farm, and provides technical assistance and training to those interested at the local, national, and international level.[2]

According to our host, who also was our teacher and tour guide, all the vegetables produced on this particular farm are 100 percent organic.[3] The Farm hosts more than 3,500 visitors a year, many of whom are affiliated with universities or scientific institutions and representing 17 countries. However, the majority of visitors come from the United States; there was even a visit from a contingent of 24 university professors who were sponsored by the New York Botanical Garden.

Our host and teacher was extremely knowledgeable about the dire effects that chemicals can have on the ecosystem in general and on human beings in particular. He cited the well-known book *Silent Spring* by Rachel Carson, published by Houghton Mifflin in 1962, as a source that the worker-farmers used as a model. He claimed that, after World War II, the various chemical companies produced 25 percent of the Earth's contamination and pointed out that humans are the "only animal that destroys their own environment." He went further to say that 10–15 million hectares (24–37 million acres) of forests are eliminated every year by the chemicals humans employ. Our host was proud to make it known that the Farm is doing whatever it can to rectify this lamentable situation, and said that the "problem of nutrition is not of production, but of political will."

### Agroecological Farming

The farmers use absolutely no chemicals for fertilizer or killing pests. On a state farm of this size, 160 tons of chemicals would be required to fertilize the land, and 30–40 tons of soil would subsequently be lost due to contamination. On an organic farm, there is no waste, and no chemicals are used or needed. This particular farm grows more than 230 species of vegetables in a relatively small space. They follow an agroecological system, a method of farming that is more environmentally friendly than the agribusinesses so common in the United States. According to agroecology.com, agroecology is:

- The application of ecology to the design and management of sustainable agroecosystems.
- A whole-systems approach to agriculture and food systems development based on traditional knowledge, alternative agriculture, and local food system experiences.
- Linking ecology, culture, economics, and society to sustain agricultural production, healthy environments, and viable food and farming communities.[4]

It is an environmentally sustainable approach to farming. Professor Stephen R. Gliessman of the Department of Environmental Studies, UC Santa Cruz, has provided the following definition of sustainable agriculture:

A whole-systems approach to food, feed, and fiber production that balances environmental soundness, social equity, and economic viability among all sectors of the public, including international and intergenerational peoples. Inherent in this definition is the idea that sustainability must be extended not only globally but indefinitely in time, and to all living organisms including humans.

Sustainable agroecosystems:

- Maintain their natural resource base.
- Rely on minimum artificial inputs from outside the farm system.
- Manage pests and diseases through internal regulating mechanisms.
- Recover from the disturbances caused by cultivation and harvest.[5]

But besides the benefits to the environment and the local people, there are many economic benefits connected with such farms, although these have been largely ignored or deemed financially unsustainable in the United States. As we have seen with the

London Symphony Orchestra, the Lusty Lady, and New Era Windows, however, alternatives are not only possible, but also sustainable. Their success depends on the conditions of existence in which they participate, and these can be threatened or compromised by powerful, "deep pocket" or monopoly capitalists. (Monsanto is one excellent example in the farming industry.)

### Prices

Many cooperatives or WSDEs in the United States are small, but there is evidence that increasing the size of cooperatives is indeed possible: consider, for example, the Mondragon Cooperatives in the Basque Region of Spain or the Evergreen Cooperatives initiative in Ohio. Cooperatives need not be limited to "boutique" worker-owned institutions. Because of the relatively small size of most of the cooperatives in the United States, the workers have a difficult time selling their goods and services since they are typically more expensive than the mass-produced commodities of major corporations. In economic terms, because of their small size, the worker cooperatives have not reached "economies of scale"; they must of necessity charge a higher price than the bigger producers because they cannot buy in bulk and therefore do not enjoy the wholesale discount that the larger firms receive. There are other kinds of "scale" problems that small firms encounter, such as advertising, specialization, technology, and even nepotism, among others. The capitalist system, whether it is state or private, is simply overwhelming and dominant and seems to have as its goal the destruction of small firms. One need only recall what happens to small local stores when a Walmart opens in the area. The small establishments cannot hope to compete because they simply do not have the power over the wholesalers that Walmart has.

Not so in Cuba. The situation is quite different there, at least on the Farm. These workers perform all the necessary tasks on the Farm, everything from composting and enriching the compost with earthworms to selling their products at their own stand on the side of the road and making deliveries to other markets as well. They not only produce the vegetables, but compost the waste and add earthworms to the compost to make the soil looser and facilitate the growth of the vegetables, and they have also found a way to extend the growing season, which in Cuba's tropical climate can last for almost the entire year. We learned that the earthworms lay their eggs in the colder months, and so the earthworms from this new generation are mature and ready to cultivate the soil as soon as the weather warms. The result is a longer growing season than on the farms that choose to use chemicals, which, incidentally, the earthworms avoid because of the "salty conditions that result from an application of chemical fertilizer."[6] Not surprisingly, the earthworms are significantly cheaper than chemicals and have the additional advantage of being able to reproduce themselves.

The Farm has only one tractor, which is very loud and also very old; our host joked about it being held together with tape (another example of the "rubber bands and paper clips" approach to vehicle maintenance). The tractor was being used sparingly while we were visiting, and our host insisted that, because of the soot it emits, this is the typical amount of use; it is used only when absolutely necessary. In an aside, he told us that the worker-farmers are also the mechanics who keep that tractor running.

According to our host, the prices for vegetable that are grown on the state farms are typically market driven, determined by the intersection of supply and demand. However, he continued, that is not the case on this Farm: since they do everything themselves, they are much more efficient than the state farms and the multinationals. Thus, the prices for the vegetables grown at the Farm are approximately 25 percent less than for those that are grown elsewhere and are not even necessarily organic.

### The Farm: Then and Now

The economic and political changes that followed the disintegration of the Soviet Bloc in the early 1990s brought about a severe crisis in Cuba. Due to the lack of imported foods, the Cuban people experienced food shortages and the state administrators determined that various "experiments" might help to keep the country sustainable and independent. Many of the state farms were divided up for local communities to run, and the Farm was one such "experiment."

The Farm was allotted approximately 800 square meters in 1997 by the Cuban government. A group of only eight workers established the Farm by building its entire infrastructure, including houses, greenhouses, protected areas for cultivation, and a center for organic fertilizer, among other projects. Within a year, crops were slowly but steadily growing. Fifteen years later, when I visited in 2012, it was thriving.

The workers had to learn from scratch how to do organic farming. Cuba had instituted a national training center to teach specialized farming, and the workers took full advantage. They also attended many conferences and workshops so that they could get the most and best training possible. The workers said that being trained and educated properly gave them "self-esteem and independence" that they had never had before. Although the workers would like to expand the Farm, there is no room to grow in their present urban location.

The Farm workers take learning on the job extremely seriously—the more experienced workers are expected to share their knowledge, wisdom, and farming know-how. They now grow enough produce for the more than 50,000 people who make purchases at their farm stand every year. The workers also share their knowledge and information about organic farming with their customers and even go into schools to give talks to the local children. The Farm is truly a community endeavor: more than 90 percent of the workers live in the local vicinity. The Farm and its cooperative members believe sincerely in community involvement, and so they have established a training center for the entire community, including training for children from about five years old.

### The Workers

Most of the 65 men and 60 women who work at the Farm have been on the job for more than three years. They are paid approximately 1,000–1,200 pesos per month, which is twice as much as the farmers on the Cuban state farms earn. On the rare occasions when there are openings for new workers, the positions are posted at the National Training Center. New workers' salaries begin at approximately 300–340 pesos per month; however, after three months on the job, their pay jumps by 540 pesos. Finally, the workers who were there from the Farm's beginning earn 1,400 pesos a month.

The workers have established the various pay scales in their bylaws, and, naturally, they are not all earning the same salaries. This was a conscious decision because of the workers' time and investment into the infrastructure at the beginning, when they worked without pay to develop the Farm and construct its buildings. But every worker after the requisite time will see his or her salary increase. And while the workers may not have equal salaries, they do have equal rights, and the voting and decision making is quite democratic. Also considered investments are the intensive training and classes required of the new cooperative members. There is no cost to the workers for these classes, and the workers, both experienced and novice, realize the importance of the training and truly understand it as a necessary preparation for their future.

As we have seen, the strict US embargo has taught the Cuban people that "necessity is the mother of invention." The workers are constantly trying to find innovative ways to optimize their extremely scarce resources. They have planning meetings simply to keep abreast of what they have and what they need. The workers can then request assistance from the Cuban administrators, but their requests must be innovative and must have a definite purpose.

When I asked about managers and leadership, I was told that these positions are open to anyone and are often rotated. There are no term limits and any worker can be a substitute at any given time. One need not be a specialist in any one area on the Farm to be a leader; most of the workers already know how to do the jobs of all the others.

One of the more interesting aspects of the working conditions on the Farm has to do with the weather in Cuba, with its tropical climate and often extremely high temperatures. With this in mind, the members collectively made the decision to decrease their working hours in the hottest summer months. From

September through May, the farmers work seven hours a day, and then in the summertime, they reduce their workday by an hour. They work five days a week, but, because of the nature of farming, which typically requires attention seven days a week, half of the workers come in for five hours on Saturdays and the other half for five hours on Sunday. They alternate their weekend days weekly, and they work from 7:00 a.m. to noon, which gives them the opportunity to be with their families for at least most of the weekend.

While this is a private farm in a Communist nation, there are some benefits that continue, even though the workers are no longer state employees. Cuba has a national health-care system that is available to all of its citizens, whether they are public or private employees. Workers at the Farm also enjoy the same pension benefits as the state workers in that they get the requisite one-month vacation per year, and they have two days off every month for personal reasons and women receive one year off with full pay for maternity leave. Indeed, as our host told us proudly, "privatization does not have to be ugly." Thus the government provides important conditions of existence to support this enterprise structure.

## State Farmers Vis-À-Vis Private Farmers

Dividing the state farms into smaller ones, and letting the worker-farmers run them as cooperatives was one of the most significant of the various Cuban "experiments." The Farm is one such experiment, and according to its workers, it has been very successful. The workers do everything for themselves and have gained a self-esteem that the state-farm workers do not while earning approximately twice the wages that their state counterparts do. Unlike workers on the state farm, the cooperative workers also work fewer hours and have the decision-making power. The Farm workers have taken ownership of their working lives and are quite happy to be productive individuals without a Communist/state capitalist boss pushing them around. The Farm credo is a perfect example of economic democracy.

As I have explained previously (Mulder, 2015), simply determining whether an organization is non-profit, for-profit, state-owned, or privately owned is insufficient in itself to distinguish the class process that is in place. Of course, these variables may compromise or reinforce the organization's conditions of existence, but they are not the defining moment. How the work is organized is the key to identifying the class process. Indeed, the workers at the Farm are toiling on state property; they do not own the land, but they do own their labor power and decide what happens to the fruits (no pun intended) of their labor. Clearly, ownership alone does not enable us to discern the mode of production of an enterprise. The workers on the state farms are told what to do, where and when to do it, and how to do it—whereas workers at the Farm make these empowering and meaningful decisions themselves. As Richard Wolff states: "Production works best when performed by a community that directly and democratically designs and carries out shared labor" (Wolff, 2012, 1–2).

## NMCA and the Farm

To find a WSDE in Cuba was something of a surprise; however, the Farm does indeed exemplify what Richard Wolff offered in his book *Democracy at Work: A Cure for Capitalism* (2012). It is the workers who collectively decide what they are going to produce, where on the Farm they will produce it, how the proceeds of the sales are distributed, and makes all decisions regarding their working conditions. Thus, these workers are not exploited. They produce the goods, vegetables, and herbs, then they appropriate any surplus generated from the sales, and then they make distributions from it to secure their conditions of existence. They do not own the land on which they work, thereby proving that ownership *does not* define a class structure.

The Farm workers occupy the two fundamental class positions as both producers and appropriators of the surplus. They also occupy the subsumed class positions as surplus distributors. The more experienced workers and those with more longevity might also hold the subsumed class position of a surplus recipient given their wages are somewhat higher than less senior workers. But the decision to give these workers the "extra" wages was made collectively and is integral to the manner in which they have chosen to operate the Farm. Of course, the workers also make payments to other recipients to secure the conditions of existence as a WSDE.

There are no bosses, and leaders are elected and rotated; the Farm is a true example of economic democracy and a WSDE.

Very much like the workers in the London Symphony Orchestra, the organization is not compromised to the extent that the Lusty Lady was and the New Era workers are. The financing of the Farm and the LSO have the support of the political, economic, and cultural forces around them. Unfortunately, this is not yet the case in the United States, but things are changing, as I will show in my concluding chapter. Momentum is building to create work organizations that are alternatives to capitalism that is failing most US workers. The latest economic crisis has led people to think about different arrangements—but words like "socialism" and "communism" are so abhorrent to most, that it is a difficult endeavor. Even so, change is not impossible. If explained as the "American Dream" of running one's own enterprise, the idea of a Worker Self-Directed Enterprise becomes much more appealing. One important note: many believe that the "American Dream" is sole ownership of a firm, but we must not forget that such enterprises frequently fail, especially the smaller ones, given the power and money that corporations wield. It also is not particularly "social," in that running one's own business can be a hard and lonely experience. Some deem this sole ownership (the ancient class process according to Resnick and Wolff, 1988 as self-exploitation. I have firsthand knowledge of this type of firm[7] and can attest that there is very little room for collective and cooperative interactions; all aspects of the business, both the good and the bad, are the responsibility of a single person, the owner. We are social beings and spend much of our lives working, and so to me at least, working collectively is a much-preferred option. As a matter of fact, capitalist workers already do work collectively, and this proves that collective labor can be successful. The regrettable fact, however, is that the workers in most firms have no control over the surplus they produce.

### Conclusion

As we have seen, Cuba was forced to overhaul its economy, along with other parts of its society, after the fall of the Soviet Union and the Eastern Bloc countries. The experiment of dividing land among the Cuban farmers seems to be quite successful and helps to negate the notion that capitalism is the most efficient and preferred economic system. As I have seen first-hand, the workers were empowered by the WSDE structure of the Farm and had a sense of self-esteem that one rarely encounters. But the Farm and the workers have state support, particularly with financing, health care, maternity leave, and public pensions, which are benefits not currently available to WSDEs or workers in the United States.

In a way, Cuba was forced into making such experiments because it no longer had favorable trade relations with the former Soviet Union and Comecon; their ready source for "diesel fuel, gasoline, trucks, agricultural machinery, spare parts for trucks and machinery, as well as the petrochemical-based fertilizer and pesticides" was suddenly gone, and these commodities became quite scarce (Koont, 2009). The urban organic farms were Cuba's answer to a crisis in food production. Even the Associated Press's June 8, 2008, headlines read, "Cuba's Urban Farming Program a Stunning Success" (ibid.). But as Koont goes on to say, these changes were not just economic; they were "also about community development and preserving and improving the environment, bringing a healthier and saner way of life to the cities" (ibid.).

Organic food sold in the United States, especially staples like milk, eggs, and bread, are considerably more expensive than the conventional products.[8] Consumers who are not in a higher income bracket are largely priced out of the market: the poor simply cannot afford the healthier organic alternatives. This is not the case in Cuba. As we have seen, the organic produce grown there is approximately 25 percent less expensive than the chemical-based traditional foods. This is partly because of the US embargo, but also because the Cuban farms are based in local communities and therefore save on shipping costs and other expenses. Perhaps with the talks about relaxing the US embargo with Cuba that are now underway, the United States may come to recognize the value of alternative approaches to food production that do not involve the use of chemicals and GMOs. What is also possible, however, given the relative size and power of the two nations and the political influence of firms like Monsanto, is that the United States will pass unhealthy agricultural techniques along to the Cubans. Time will tell. What we do know is that the Cuban farmers have shown us that WSDEs are not only possible, but sustainable and environmentally friendly as well.

# CHAPTER 6

# The Green Bay Packers: "A Love Story between a Community and a Team"[1]

## Introduction

The Green Bay Packers are celebrated as being "community owned and operated," but is that really the case? Indeed, the media and literature would lead you to believe that the Packers are the epitome of socialism, even "an anarchist organization" that is neither publicly nor privately owned (Peppe, 2015). In his article in the online political newsletter *Counterpunch*, Matt Peppe states that the Packers use "an anarcho-syndicalist model, similar to workers taking control of the factory and running it democratically" like the New Era workers whom we encountered in Chapter 4. This is a seriously misleading statement. Moreover, even Dave Zirin's article in *The New Yorker* states that "Green Bay stands as a living, breathing, and, for the [other NFL teams'] owners, frightening example, that pro sports can aid our cities in tough economic times, not drain them of scarce resources" (Zirin, 2011).

It is true that the Packers are publicly owned and have been since 1923. The "[f]ans have supported the team financially through five stock sales: 1923, 1935, 1950, 1997, and 2011" (2014 Packers Media Guide). There are currently 360,584 shareholders, with 5,011,557 outstanding shares. But while the Packers have many philanthropic causes, as the analysis below will show, the team is a capitalist firm, organized and operated much like the other 31 teams in the National Football League (NFL), even though it is a non-profit enterprise. Known to many as the "Green Bay Clause," the NFL bylaws clearly state that no other team will be permitted to be a non-profit or charitable organization.[2] As I have written elsewhere, whether a firm is privately or publicly owned, or whether it is a non-profit or for-profit enterprise, is not significant for NMCA. The analysis considers instead the mode of production it employs (Mulder, 2015).

The relationship between the team and the community is indeed a love story, however, and that community includes not only the city, but the county and state as well. The relationship is mutual, and both the community and the Packers organization are dedicated to maintaining it. Indeed, during his opening remarks at the annual shareholders' meeting on July 24, 2013, and in a subsequent interview with me, Packers President and CEO Mark Murphy stated that the organization's mission is twofold: to win Super Bowls and to ensure that the team stays in Green Bay.[3] Almost everywhere you look in Green Bay, you are reminded that the Packers reside there and are a dearly loved institution.

## Green Bay, Wisconsin

Green Bay is the smallest community with a team in the NFL, and for that matter in any of the professional sports organizations in the United States (Nadeau and Thompson, 1996, 125). According to the latest US census, the city has a population of approximately 105,000, with a median household income of $42,427 and a poverty rate of almost 20 percent.[4] It is a small city with a huge 80,000-seat stadium in the middle of it, almost big enough to hold the entire city. Unlike other NFL stadiums, Lambeau Field sits adjacent to many small single-family homes. In the summer, the weather in Green Bay is quite nice, but the winters are notoriously harsh—however, even the latest renovations at Lambeau Field did not include the installation of a roof (dome). The Green Bay residents I queried said that adding a dome would be "sacrilegious" and would be too great a departure from tradition, even though their city has the coldest winters in the NFL.[5] It is a lovely Midwestern community that is in love with its Packers, as even a quick drive around the city will demonstrate. There is even a section of the city known as "Titletown," in honor of the Packers' 13 NFL championship titles.

The Packers put the northern Wisconsin city of Green Bay on the map and have kept it there. Without the Packers, it would be like any other obscure city in the Midwest, known mainly to those who live in or near it. Other NFL franchises often hold communities "hostage" with their credible threats to abandon a city for more lucrative markets unless they are given subsidies, tax breaks, or new stadiums (often paid for with public dollars); the offer of a new stadium to an existing team may be quite enticing and can easily initiate a struggle between communities. For example, the Los Angeles area has been without a professional football team since the Rams moved to St. Louis approximately twenty years ago. Roger Goodell, the president of the NFL, now seems willing to increase the number of teams in the league by two—there would be scheduling problems if only one team were added—and now that an 80,000-seat state-of-the-art stadium will be built in Inglewood, not far from Los Angeles, the City of Angels may once again be home to an NFL team.[6] On the other hand, should there not be two new teams, Inglewood/Los Angeles might make lucrative offers to an existing team; thus, that team would abandon the community in which they are presently. The Packers, however, can never be lured away from Green Bay because of their unique arrangement with the city.

## The Packers

It is commonly assumed that the city of Green Bay owns the Packers,[7] but, according to the Director of the Green Bay Economic Development Association, Greg Flisram, Packers shareholders hail from all fifty states, US territories, and now Canada.[8] Another erroneous assumption is that the Packers pay no federal taxes because they are a non-profit enterprise, but they are in fact exempt only from Wisconsin state taxes. Because of federal regulations, the organization does not qualify as a registered 501(c)(3) charity: organizations with shareholders are ineligible for 501(c)(3) status and must pay federal taxes.[9] On the other hand, according to Aaron Popkey,[10] the Packers Public Relations Director, "Wisconsin realized the Packers' benefits to the State" and thus designated the team as a non-profit at the state level. The Packers, he said, are not only Green Bay's team, but also Wisconsin's team. Moreover, the Brown County voters elected in 1997 to implement a half-cent sales tax to support the Packers; thus, like most of the other 31 NFL teams, but on a much smaller scale, the Packers receive contributions from the taxpayers in their hometown.

Green Bay is an interesting place to visit in that almost everything celebrates the "Packers," even the city buses, which are painted with the team's colors. The major tourist attraction is Lambeau Field, named for Packers' founder Earl "Curly" Lambeau and located on Lombardi Street, which was named for their infamous coach, Vince Lombardi. Unlike other NFL stadiums, the name of the stadium in Green Bay is not that of a corporate sponsor. It does, however, have many corporate sponsors, including "gate sponsors." Every gate (entrance/exit) at Lambeau Field is named for a particular corporate sponsor. Lambeau Field is in fact commercialized just like other stadiums of other NFL teams.[11] The Packers maintain the stadium, but the land is owned by the city and the Green Bay/Brown County Professional Football District (2013 Media Guide, 576). It is currently the third largest arena in the NFL with over 80,000 seats.[12] (Appendix A summarizes each NFL stadium's capacity.)

Although the team usually hosts only ten home games in the course of the NFL season, the Packers and the city have made Lambeau Field into a 363-day-a-year operation, closing only on Christmas and Easter.[13] The stadium's "atrium" and other spaces are rented out for a number of different events year round, anything from a corporate meeting to a formal wedding. The Packers also receive revenues from stadium tours offered for a fee, a pro shop that is the most successful in the NFL, restaurants, and the Green Bay Packers Hall of Fame—which includes an exact replica of Lombardi's office, the Packers' Vince Lombardi trophies (for their Super Bowl victories), Lombardi's Super Bowl rings, statues of the team in action, and a host of other memorabilia. In downtown Green Bay, there is a Packers' Heritage Trail—modeled after

Boston's Freedom Trail. Just about every store, restaurant, and business (even the public library) either sells Packers paraphernalia or pays homage in some way. For example, outside of the Titletown Brewery, there is a larger-than-life statue of the famous Green Bay player, Donald Driver.

The Packers organization has also made various investments to attract tourists other than on game days. Indeed, its economic impact is quite significant. According to a recent thorough study by AECOM Technical Services, Inc (AECOM), the "impact of the Packers and the renovated Lambeau Field on the community" was estimated at $281.5 million in 2009 (2013 Media Guide, 110). They are currently in the midst of a two-phase $285 million expansion of Lambeau Field, for which they proudly state that "no funding [is] from public tax money" (2013 Media Guide, 578). The first phase is now complete and the completion of the second phase is expected in 2015. The funding for these endeavors came from a stock sale, two loans from the NFL, and from the "stadium district." One really has to visit Green Bay to truly understand not only the Packers' economic impact, but also the team's all-encompassing relationship with the city and county. It is almost infectious.

It is important to note, however, that the Packers organization invests in the community in a number of different ways, not only by attracting tourists, but also by giving to mainly Green Bay and Wisconsin charities.[14] While the Packers are well known for their varied and extensive philanthropic efforts, they also continuously expand their investment in profitable ventures, most recently in the form of a long-term lease to Cabela's, an extensive outdoor sporting goods chain store located on Packers' property. According to Murphy there are plans that are yet to be announced to rent the surrounding property to other ventures, including restaurants, retail stores, and possibly a luxury hotel.[15] Although he would not reveal the details, lease agreement, or other project, Murphy did say that the Packers organization is currently in negotiations and looking for potential interest [capitalist] businesses. Leasing the land will no doubt yield profits, all of which will go back into the Packers organization for salaries, stadium maintenance, and charitable endeavors since, as Packers President Mark Murphy points out, "[the Packers organization] does not have the profit motive" like every other NFL team. The relationship between the Packers and Green Bay (including Brown County) is absolutely a mutually beneficial one—it is the proverbial two-way street.

## What Makes the Packers Unique?

The Packers are legally bound to Green Bay and, unlike the other 31 NFL teams, cannot simply move their operations to another city or venue. According to their own bylaws, until the late 1990s, if the team were purchased and moved away, any profits earned from the sale would go to the Sullivan Post of the American Legion in Green Bay. Moreover, if "there [should] be a dissolution of The Green Bay Packers, the players shall be subject to the National Football League Rules and become free agents, but the undivided profits and assets of The Green Bay Packers, Inc., shall go to the Sullivan Post of the American Legion for the purpose of creating a proper soldiers' memorial either by building, clubhouse, hospital or other charitable or educational program." In 1997, this clause was changed, and now the proceeds would go to the Green Bay Packers Foundation, a charitable trust. As the quotation from the NFL bylaws at the beginning of this chapter states, no other team may enjoy the same organizational model as Green Bay. The article is commonly referred to as the "Green Bay Clause," but it does not apply to the Packers because the team was *grandfathered* in. One might well wonder why this clause was so crucial, and why the other NFL team owners should care what any team's leaders do with their profits.

As we have seen, the Packers are a registered non-profit entity in Wisconsin but are subject to federal taxes. In 2010, for example, the Packers paid $2.5 million.[16] But why should a book about cooperative enterprises and transforming capitalism include a case study of the Green Bay Packers, a multi-million-dollar National Football League team, the winner of the most NFL world championships with 13, whose players (workers) earn million-dollar salaries? The answer is quite simple: because it is a "unique" enterprise in at least three aspects of its structure and operation that can clearly be analyzed within the NMCA framework. First, while they are considered a non-profit, charitable organization in their home state, and will retain that status unless there is a significant change to the NFL bylaws, its class structure is capitalist. Secondly, it is publicly owned, whereas a single owner has a majority interest in every other NFL team. And finally, the Packers' Articles of Incorporation specify that the team must remain in Green Bay, thereby providing this small community with a significant revenue stream, one that is critical for its economy. Unlike other schools of economic thought, NMCA has the tools needed to analyze the internal and external contradictions inherent in the organizational structure of the Packers.

The Packers stay in Green Bay, bucking the trend of the other NFL teams, because, if the team left, the franchise would dissolve. This gives the franchise some room to grow or to take risks that other coaches and teams might not take. Murphy, for example, decided not to rehire Brett Favre, the Green Bay star quarterback, when he came back from retirement, hiring instead a relatively unknown quantity, Aaron Rogers. And they can afford to stay in Green Bay because they do not have to worry about being profitable; they need only be sustainable. Furthermore, according to Public Relations Director Aaron Popkey, remaining in Green Bay is possible thanks to the television revenue-sharing proviso in the NFL bylaws[17] and the "salary cap" included in the collective-bargaining agreement between the NFL and the players' union, the National Football League Players Association (NFLPA).[18] Popkey went on to say that NFL teams in smaller markets do not bring in as large a television revenue as those in a major market like New York. If the smaller-market teams did not receive a proportionate amount of the revenues, they would fail financially, thus threatening the viability of the entire league. If the teams in the smaller markets fold, then there would be fewer teams for the remaining ones to play—eventually dismantling the NFL. Popkey further explained that the salary cap eliminates the unfair advantage that the more profitable teams or those with "deep pocket" owners would have. Moreover, if the Packers were to need funds, the team would have to get the NFL's permission to sell more stock. That is unlikely according to Murphy, barring a need for capital improvements to Lambeau Stadium.

## History

The Packers, established in 1919 by Earl "Curly" Lambeau, had a troubled first few years. They had three owners between 1919 and 1923. At one point, the Packers were thrown out of the American Professional Football Association (APFA) for using college players.[19] However, Lambeau, dedicated to making the Packers successful, was able to have the team reinstated into the APFA before the 1922 season. After failed fund-raising attempts and facing bankruptcy, Lambeau and four businessmen decided to go public, that is, to sell shares of stock in the franchise and reorganize it into a non-profit whose net revenues would go to a local American Legion post (Nadeau and Thompson, 1996, 126). The post is now known as the Sullivan-Wallen American Legion Post 11. Although no longer the heir to the Packers, the post still has strong ties to the team. In fact, the Legion's color guard has carried the American flag for every home game since the 1940s. The community, especially the returning veterans from World War I, rallied around the Packers (ibid.). In 1923 at a local Elks club, the five men sold 1,000 shares of stock for $5 each (Belson, 2011, B17), and the Green Bay Packers Corporation was formed.

Struggling again financially in the midst of the Great Depression, the Packers were forced to reorganize and sell more shares of stock. As with the first offering, the fans rallied and the Packers raised $15,000 from the second sale. The new Green Bay Packers, Inc., was now formed. In the new articles of incorporation, the same American Legion post would receive the proceeds from the sale of any assets:

> This corporation shall be non-profit sharing and its purposes shall be exclusively for charitable purposes, the profits, if any, to be donated to the Sullivan Post of the American Legion, or other war veterans' organizations, the stockholders not to receive any dividend or pecuniary profit (*Articles of Incorporation of the Green Bay Packers (Articles)*, Article III, 1935, 2).

This ensured that the team would remain in Green Bay, which was critical to those who purchased the shares. Had the Packers not been willing to make this concession, they would have gone bankrupt.

The Articles of Incorporation were furthermore amended in 1937 so that the Sullivan Post would no longer be the sole recipient; contributions could also be made to the "Community Chest or other local charitable institutions proportional to the other Green Bay institutions . . ." (*Articles*, Article VI, 1937, 2). The 1937 articles went even further to say that "should there be a dissolution of The Green Bay Packers, Inc., the players shall be subject to the National Football League Rules and become free agents, but the undivided profits and assets of The Green Bay Packers, Inc., shall go to the Sullivan[20] Post of the American Le-tion for the purpose of creating a proper soldiers' memorial either by building, clubhouse, hospital, or other charitable or educational program." (ibid.). This remained in force until 1997, when the Packers once again voted to amend their bylaws, making the Green Bay Packers Foundation, a charitable entity, the recipient of revenues from the sale of any assets.[21] As Aaron Popkey and I walked to Lambeau Field for the shareholders' annual meeting, he told me that the former Packers' CEO Bob Harlan used to quip that, if the Packers ceased to exist, the Green Bay High School would have the best local football field in the country.[22]

## NMCA and the Green Bay Packers

Even given its quasi-non-profit status, the Green Bay Packers organization is a capitalist enterprise within the NMCA framework. The focus of the NMCA project is the elimination of exploitation—which the Packers have no intention of doing. But the organization is nonetheless important for our study because of the benefits to the community: revenues from tourism, the Packers' charitable contributions, and, more importantly, the ancillary effects, such as theater, arts, museums, an arena that hosts concerts and the like, and a vibrant farmers' market and downtown area, among others. Green Bay/Brown County also seem to have avoided much of the hemorrhaging in the manufacturing sector that most other Midwest cities have suffered over the last thirty years. The major manufacturing employers include Proctor & Gamble, multiple paper mills, packaging plants, agribusiness (particularly dairy products), and the largest industry in Green Bay, the health-care sector. The Packers themselves have multiple employees, but are not a major employer of local residents. Indeed, although some of the players have made entrepreneurial endeavors in the community, most of them have their main residences somewhere else and only reside in Green Bay for the season. The concession stands at Lambeau Field are run by charitable organizations, and they are "manned" by volunteers. Volunteers also do many of the "chores" around the stadium, and there never seems to be a shortage of them. For example, volunteers are asked to remove the snow from the field on game days.

## Shareholders (Owners)

Since April 18, 1923, the Packers have been a shareholder-owned, non-profit corporation in Wisconsin (Green Bay Packers Media Guide, 2013, 4). In all those years, they have issued shares of stock on only five occasions, the first three to keep the team solvent and the last two for capital improvements. The current NFL bylaws stipulate that share sales can be made only for capital improvements and not because of insolvency or bankruptcy. In order to make the first (1923) sale successful, the Packers had to convince the people of Green Bay that they would remain there indefinitely; thus, the American Legion post was made the beneficiary of any profits from a sale of the team and each shareholder was required to purchase six season tickets. The last two stock offerings were for capital improvements to Lambeau Field, the third biggest in the NFL and now considered the best "stadium experience" in the league. For the 1997 and 2011 offerings, permission had to be granted by the NFL, which no longer allows shares of a team to be sold in order to avoid bankruptcy. In fact, the NFL bylaws require that there be a primary *private* owner. Nevertheless, the NFL did permit the Packers organization to make capital improvements with the proceeds of the share sales. Susan Finco, a member of the board of the directors, explained in an interview with me that they had to appeal to the NFL for permission to

**Table 6.1**   Green Bay Packers Outstanding Shares and Value

|  | Number of Shares Available for Sale | Share Price | Maximum Amount Any One Person Can Own | Total Amount Raised (Approximate) |
|---|---|---|---|---|
| 1923 | 1,000 | $5 | 200 | $5,000 |
| 1935 | 600 | $25 | 300 | $15,000 |
| 1950 | 5000 | $25 | 10,000 | $118,000 |
| 1997 | 120,010 | $200 | 200,000 | $24,000,000 |
| 2011 | 269,000 | $250 | 200,000 | $64,000,000 |

Source: 2014 Media Guide, pages 538–539.

raise money through a stock offering because, unlike the other teams, they "don't have an owner with deep pockets."[23] Table 6.1 summarizes the five share sales.

The Packers' stockholders receive no dividends and cannot really sell their shares unless they sell them back to the Packers organization, and then for only pennies on the dollar, specifically $0.025;[24] however, they can gift them to close relatives or bequeath them. This enables the Packers to remain a non-profit enterprise. No individual shareholder may own more than 200,000 shares to prevent anyone from having controlling interest. (The current average is fourteen shares per owner.) Why would anyone make a financial investment in the Packers, when no return can be expected except for a stock certificate? Traditional economists and financial planners would say that this is irrational behavior. The proud owners who flocked to Lambeau Field on July 24, 2013, do not think so. As announced at the shareholders' meeting that I attended that day, there were over 13,000 "owners" present. And, according to Packers Secretary Daniel Ariens' quorum report, 1,637,577 votes were cast for the board of directors, either in person or by proxy.

The only benefits shareholders receive are a paper stock certificates,[25] an invitation to attend the annual shareholder's meeting at Lambeau Field, a vote per share on the board of directors, and "bragging rights." As will be further discussed below, even though shareholders have voting rights, the election is typically a *fait accompli* by the time of the voting like so many other big US corporations. The

current board members vet potential new members for their particular skills, connections, or status and they usually run unopposed.
I understand from the many people I spoke with during my trip to
Green Bay in July 2013 that almost everyone in the town, possibly
in the county, has a framed Packers' stock certificate on their home
or office wall. Indeed, special frames for these certificates can be
purchased in the pro shop at Lambeau Field, at a cost of between
$89.95 and $139.[26] The Packers fans not only support their team
by rooting for them at game time, they also support them with
their dollars when they buy shares, which on each occasion sold out
rather quickly. Some would ask, "[W]hy would buyers be interested
in stock that has none of the advantages of traditional stock, and
where buyers are warned that they 'should not purchase common
stock with the purpose of making a profit'? Because it gives them
a vote. Because of history. Because it's their town. Because it's their
team" (Couple of Sports.com).[27]

The shareholders, in their positions as owners hold no class
positions within the NMCA methodology. They have no direct
relationship with the players in their capacity as surplus value producing workers, that is, they cannot hire/fire players, nor can they
fine them or give them instructions about how to do their jobs
more efficiently; thus, they do *not* occupy a fundamental class position as appropriator. Moreover, although they purchase shares of
Packers stock and provide much-needed revenue to the team, they
do not hold a subsumed class position because they receive neither
dividends nor any tangible (fiduciary) benefits from their ownership status. This demonstrates that within the NMCA framework,
ownership of the means of production and the ability to hire/fire
workers is *insufficient* evidence of the particular class process in
effect at a site of production. Ownership may provide conditions
of existence, as it did in the other cases we have considered, but
the Packers shareholders occupy only non-class positions.

## Board of Directors

The relationship between the shareholders and the board of directors is much like that in most other public enterprises: the shareholders elect the board members but do not have control over

the operation of the team (the "enterprise"). The Packers board of directors has a maximum of 45 members, "not less than five (5) to have residence outside the County of Brown, nor more than fifteen (15)" (Packers Bylaws, 3). (This residency requirement further ensures that the Packers will not leave Green Bay because the resident directors have a vested interest in keeping them there.) In actuality, Director Susan Finco said, the board members are selected by other board members for their particular expertise, connections, and/or skills, and, by the time of the annual shareholders' meeting, the new board members have already been selected and announced. The board then elects its Chairman, who may or may not also be the President. (Mark Murphy is currently both CEO and President.) Board members are elected for three-year terms on a rotating basis, that is, one-third of the board members' terms end each year. The President and CEO represent the Packers "owners" in negotiations with the Players' Union as well as with the NFL. With the exception of the CEO and President, board members receive no compensation for their participation.

Each member of the board of directors occupies both a fundamental class position, and some also occupy subsumed class positions. As the first surplus recipients, they occupy the fundamental class position as appropriator of the surplus created by the players, though they do not receive payments for this position. The entire board makes the surplus distribution decisions. Many board members also occupy a subsumed class position in that their firms or personal talents are employed to ensure the Packers' conditions of existence; for example, board members might own marketing and real estate firms, providing services for which the Packers pay. If board members receive payments for their services to the Packers, those payments are for their roles as a subsumed class occupants. Board members who receive no such payments do not occupy a subsumed class position.

## The Executive Committee

The board of directors elects seven of its members to the Packers' Executive Committee (EC).[28] The EC "directs corporate management, approves major capital expenditures, establishes broad policy and monitors management's performance in conducting the business and affairs of the corporation" (Media Guide, (2013), 28). The EC is currently composed of Mark Murphy (President), Larry Weyers (Vice President), Mark McMullen (Treasurer), Daniel Ariens (Secretary), and three members at large—Thomas Olejniczak, John Bergstrom, and Thomas Olson.

Except for CEO Mark Murphy, the Executive Committee members receive no salaries or payments for their work. As the board of directors' representatives, they hold a fundamental class position as surplus value appropriators, even more directly than the full board. They make distributions from the surplus value in the form of federal taxes, premiums for star players, front office employees, and talent scouts, and dues to the NFL, among other payments. Thus, they also hold the subsumed class position as surplus value distributors.

## The Coaching Staff

The Packers coaching staff members work at the behest of the board and its EC. The coaches are much like the conductors referred to in the London Symphony Orchestra chapter. The coaches organize, instruct, and much like a symphony conductor, ensure that the workers are harmonious. In these roles, the coaching staff produces surplus value, and thus they occupy fundamental class positions. They do not, however, appropriate or distribute the surplus value, and so they are considered exploited workers within the NMCA methodology.

Conversely, the coaches are also the eyes and ears of the EC and the CEO as supervisors. In this capacity, they do not occupy fundamental class positions because they are not producing or appropriating surplus value, but they do occupy subsumed class positions as surplus value recipients by ensuring that surplus value is produced by the workers, including the coaching staff. Head coach Mike McMurray answers directly to CEO Mark Murphy and the other coaching staff report to McMurray. For these positions, the coaches receive a surplus distribution, but do not distribute the surplus value themselves. Thus, they hold only a subsumed class position as surplus value recipients. It must be obvious that the coaches are vital to the organization and earn the salaries and prestige that come with their positions (Mulder, 2009).

## The Front Office and Other Staff

As with the office staff at the London Symphony Orchestra, the Packers have a considerable number of people working in their front offices (mostly at Lambeau Field, their headquarters). These positions include: Administration, Finance, Human Resources, Public Relations, Packers Media Group & Brand Engagement, Marketing, Information Technology, Community Outreach, Packers Pro Shop, Stadium Services, Ticketing, Facilities and Fields, Security, Football Operations, Player Personnel (scouts), Video, Equipment, and Medical. These workers are critical to the smooth operation of the Green Bay Packers; if they were not—that is, if their positions were redundant—they would not be employed. These workers ensure that revenues are generated, whether in the form of surplus value or through other revenue streams. For example, the medical staff confirms whether or not a player is physically capable of producing the surplus value, and in return they receive a distribution of the surplus value for their work. They are not producing, appropriating, or distributing surplus value and thus are not exploited workers, but they do hold subsumed class positions as recipients.

On the other hand, the workers in the pro shop sell Packers paraphernalia such as jerseys and other mementos. These workers are not producing anything new; they are not transforming the raw materials and capital with their labor power into something more valuable and are not the first recipient of the surplus value. The pro shop managers hold this position and receive a subsumed class payment for operating the store. The workers, who are similar to those in any other retail establishment (Mulder, 2011), do nothing to ensure that the players are producing surplus value, but they do facilitate a significant revenue stream for the Packers organization, which of course helps the organization to remain solvent.

## The National Football League

The National Football League is the primary "trade organization" of professional football in the United States. Its members are all 32 professional teams, who pay a total of approximately $250–300 million in membership dues each year,[29] about $10.2 million per team.[30] The NFL is a registered 501(c)(6) that acts much like a chamber of commerce. The statute is written in such a way that the NFL is protected from violating the Sherman Anti-Trust Act, which makes it illegal to operate a monopoly—although that is what the NFL does. However, according to the Internal Revenue Service an "IRC 501(c)(6) provides for exemption of business leagues, chambers of commerce, real estate boards, boards of trade, and professional football leagues (whether or not administering a pension fund for football players), which are not organized for profit and no part of the net earnings of which inures to the benefit of any private shareholder or individual."[31] The primary functions of the NFL are that it:

> [E]stablishes rules and practices for its members by hiring game referees and considering competitive rule changes every offseason. It develops ways for the organization to run more efficiently and profitably by setting up the college draft, conducting player safety research, and negotiating collective bargaining agreements between the Players' Union and the team owners. It also promotes the business in the broader community by running youth football camps, giving to charities, and setting up big game-promoting events like the Super Bowl. (Blitz, 2014)[32]

It is much like a trade union of team owners. Since Green Bay has over 5 million owners, Packers CEO Mark Murphy represents them in the NFL. Of late there has been much said about the non-profit status the NFL currently enjoys, particularly when League Commissioner Roger Goodell's salary and bonuses in his first seven years totaled approximately $123 million, with large increases coming after the NFL teams "locked out" their players in 2011. In 2013 alone, Goodell took in $44.2 million, a 300-percent increase from his first year (Gaines, 2008).[33]

Membership in the NFL is required for all 32 teams; otherwise, they would have no one to play against, and thus each team's dues are considered a subsumed class payment to ensure their conditions of existence as a professional team. To be sure, these dues, much like the union dues the players pay to the NFL Players Association (NFLPA) are tax deductions for each team. The NFL also makes loans to its members and not only sets the rules of the game, but also determines how revenues are divided. For example, all of the television revenues collected for selling airtime for the games is divided equally among the 32 teams; in the 2013/2014 season alone, approximately $6 billion was split, and each team received $187.7 million.[34] This does not include $1 billion from DirectTV, which is currently in negotiations with the league (ibid.). Given that Green Bay has the smallest television market in the league, the Packers rely on this revenue-sharing scheme; it secures the team's conditions of existence. This is also true with other teams that are not in high-market zones, such as Minnesota and Jacksonville. If the TV revenues were received by the home-team market alone, there would be far fewer NFL teams—and Green Bay probably would be among those that would dissolve. Thus, within the NMCA framework, the $10.2 million in dues assures annual television revenues of $187.7 million. The revenues are more than 18 times the dues the team paid.[35] Of this amount, according to the NFL-NFLPA collective-bargaining agreement, the players (workers) receive 55 percent of the TV revenues. This revenue-sharing scheme was just added into the latest collective-bargaining agreement, and the owners, including Packers CEO Mark Murphy, point to this fact as proof that the collective-bargaining agreement is working.[36]

### The Workers (The Green Bay Packers Players)

Like the LSO musicians, the workers are called "players." I find the use of the word player instead of worker somewhat problematic because it leads one to believe that these workers must be having fun because they are playing, not working. That is most certainly not the case. Professional football players are the surplus value producing workers who are paid wages, bonuses, and often premiums. The seventy players on each of the 32 teams produce the commodity—football games. It is interesting to note the language used, which often leads people external to football and other professional sports to get an ambiguous picture of what is happening in this workplace. The workers are called "players" and the commodity they produce is called "a game." This can lead to some erroneous beliefs about what these grown men, typically with college educations, are actually doing when "they play a game." They are not children playing hopscotch in the street for fun; they are indeed working and producing surplus value. To be completely accurate, one should refer to the game as a commodity, and to the players as workers. Without them, there would be no product. They are in fact union workers represented by the NFL Players Association (NFLPA), which is part of the 52-million-member AFL-CIO.[37] As such, they have an over 300-page collective-bargaining agreement that was negotiated between the League and their elected union representatives.

Unlike the other case studies in this book, the Green Bay Packers are unambiguously a capitalist institution. The surplus value producers are the players/workers who produce a commodity, a football game, and, even though they are highly paid, sometimes well into the millions of dollars per year, within the NMCA framework the players are exploited workers. The League and Union negotiate a "minimum" wage (as is also true for Broadway musicians; see Mulder, 2009), and they also negotiate a "salary cap." The league minimum annual salary for a rookie (first year) player in 2015 is $435,000, and the minimum is $570,000 for a veteran player (not including bonuses and other premiums).[38] The new collective-bargaining agreement also dictates a maximum of $133 million (the "salary cap") that a team can pay collectively to all its players.[39] Appendix F lists the Packers' current salaries.

The players occupy the fundamental class position as surplus value producers, but not as appropriators. The board of directors holds the fundamental class position as appropriator and also the subsumed class position of surplus value distributors. That is, the board of directors makes the decisions about surplus value payments. These payments ensure the smooth operation or the enterprise, or in other words secure its conditions of existence.

Proudly announced at the 2013 shareholders' meeting was the re-signing of Aaron Rogers and Clay Matthews, who CEO Mark Murphy said are "arguably the best offensive and defensive players in the league." Although he did not announce the salaries of these two players—which is hardly surprising given the income status of the average Green Bay owner sitting in the stands—the Green Bay Packers' salaries are public information. Both Rogers and Matthews signed five-year contracts; Rogers's contract is for $110 million, averaging $22 million annually with a guaranteed minimum of $54 million, and Matthews's contract is for $66 million, $13.2 million annually with a guarantee of $20.5 million.[40]

It may be difficult to see how NFL surplus-value-producing players are exploited, but that is indeed the case. Since it is not the workers who appropriate and distribute the surplus they produce, NMCA considers them exploited. It also may be difficult to "feel sorry" for these multi-million-dollar workers, but we must remember that many of them have a very short working life in a dangerous industry. In fact, the eldest player on the Packers team is 32 years old. The NFL salaries are admittedly quite high, but, if the team owners did not find ownership profitable and were not collecting a surplus from the workers, they would not be in the business for very long. (Appendix D lists the owners—a group that is sometimes called a billionaires club—and their net worth.) The Packers' reported profit of $25.5 million in the 2013/2014 season does not, however, go to the owners of the team, like the profits of the other 32 teams, but goes instead into either a capital reserve fund or the charitable Green Bay Foundation.

### The Union: The NFL Players Association

Like most other unions, and as we saw in Chapter 4 on the New Era Cooperative, unions often do well at resisting the encroachment of capital, but they typically do not do anything to change the mode of production. This is the case with the NFLPA as well. While they negotiate an extremely detailed collective-bargaining agreement, represent the players in contract violations through the grievance procedure, and monitor the teams' adherence to the contract, to date there has been no move by the union to facilitate eradicating the exploitation the workers endure. There is a cultural barrier that maintains the status quo, and the players and their union representatives simply do not try to take over their enterprise. Perhaps one reason for this can be found in the high salaries, but they might possibly earn even higher salaries and better treatment if the 31 owners and the Green Bay board via its CEO were not appropriating the surplus value they produced. To summarize, there is not now, and to my knowledge has never been, any evidence of the workers/players controlling their own work environment.

## The Lockout: A Contradiction?

My interest in the Packers was sparked by the 2011 lockout initiated by the NFL owners. I was particularly fascinated by what I thought was a contradiction, in that many of the Packers "owners" are themselves union members and workers, who now found themselves on the other side of the bargaining table. However, when I interviewed Packers CEO Mark Murphy, I discovered that, as the Chairman of the Board, he represents the over 300,000 Packers owners at the bargaining table and that he had no problem acting in the same capacity as the other 31 team owners, even though he himself was not only a former NFL player/worker, but had also been a business agent for the NFLPA. He said that, after more than twenty years in management, he did not see his position as problematic or contradictory. He also said that he is treated just like any other owner in the NFL, except that he does not have to worry about the "profit incentive" as the other owners do. Public Relations Director Aaron Popkey told me that, in his opinion, Mr. Murphy would do what was best for the NFL because what is good for the NFL is also good for the Green Bay Packers.

It was the Green Bay and Brown County residents and businesses who feared the lockout. The economic impact from the loss of the ten Packers' home games and the residual effects would have been a source of great distress to the community. There would have been serious economic losses in the other markets, too, but the impact would not have been nearly as great as would have been experienced in Green Bay, the smallest market.[41] Clearly, the residents of Brown County, Wisconsin, are well aware of the economic benefits the Packers provide to their community. They prove this in multiple ways: fences near Lambeau field are painted with Packers colors and words of support, Packers flags fly from many homes, there is a long waiting list for seats for Packers games, fans pay a license fee for a stadium seat (in addition to the cost of the ticket), they turn out in droves for the shareholders' meeting and even "tailgate" prior to and after the meeting, they patronize the very successful pro shop, in both its brick and mortar and its online incarnations; the list can go on and on. What surprised me most, however, was learning about the "referendum," as it is known to Brown County residents. Mary Jane Herber, the Brown County librarian/historian, explained to me that it was a Brown County referendum to raise the sales tax by ½ cent to help finance the renovations of the Packers' stadium.[42] The referendum passed on September 12, 2000. It is a rare occasion when voters elect to increase their tax burden—but that is exactly what happened in Brown County.[43]

### The Green Bay Packers Foundation

The primary difference between the Packers and a typical capitalist firm, including the other 31 NFL teams, and that is the team's non-profit status. Indeed, as we now know, the NFL bylaws specifically state that all teams must be for profit. The Packers are exempt from this requirement because their structure was in place before the bylaw change, and so they were "grandfathered in." In 1986, Packers President Robert Parins established The Green Bay Packers Foundation. The foundation is a charitable 501(c)(3), "a vehicle to assure continued contributions to charity."[44] According to its website, the foundation:

> [C]onsiders grant requests from charities possessing one or more of the following goals while raising the awareness of the Packers organization as a committed and contributing member of the various communities:
>
> • Perpetuates a community environment that promotes families and the competitive value of athletics;
> • Contributes to player and fan welfare;

- Ensures the safety and education of children; and/or
- Prevents cruelty to animals

All grantees must be "physically located" in Wisconsin and must be non-profit entities that are classified by the IRS as a 501(c)(3). In 2014, the foundation granted a total of $600,000 to 223 organizations.[45] More importantly, if the Packers were sold, the proceeds would go directly to the Foundation in accordance with the Green Bay Packers bylaws.[46]

## Conclusion

The Green Bay and Brown County, Wisconsin, communities have a professional football team—unlike any other small American town. The team's own bylaws make it clear that they cannot move and that they are a non-profit entity. They are shareholder owned by over 360,000 people, whose only reward for their ownership is a stock certificate that cannot be traded on the open market and on which no dividends are paid. Unlike the other 31 NFL stadiums, Green Bay's Lambeau Field has no "owner's box." Stock ownership does not even guarantee a shareholder a ticket to any of the games—which are sold out indefinitely.

There have been only five share offerings, the first three to keep the Packers solvent and avoid bankruptcy. The NFL subsequently changed its bylaws, prohibiting any future such sale. However, the Packers were allowed to have two more share offerings, with the proceeds used exclusively for capital improvements to Lambeau Field. By the time this book appears, all of the improvements should be completed. When I asked Mark Murphy whether there would be more, his response was, "Not that I can foresee."

Like other teams, the Packers (including the individual players) are quite philanthropic. They contribute to and participate in many charity events. The Packers differ from the other teams, because their charitable activities are confined to Green Bay, Brown County, and Wisconsin, as mandated by their bylaws. The players are accessible to the people of Green Bay, and they have fun traditions that the players and the community love. For example, many young boys and girls ride their bicycles to the Packers' practice field and the players "borrow" their bikes to go back to the locker room.

The Packers, a team that continues to attract world-class players, is the oldest team in the NFL and holds the most Super Bowl championships. Indeed, Green Bay won the first two Super Bowls, in 1967 and 1968. Given that the city is so small, with a population of only about 100,000, the Packers are very much a part of the community, and the residents are their biggest fans. The Packers' organizational structure and its relationship with its surplus value producing employees are consistent with the other teams. The Packers' organization is a NFL member, it pays NFL dues, and pays their players like any other players in the league.

What puzzled me while doing the research for this chapter was why the other 31 owners would take issue with the Packers being a non-profit, publicly owned firm. They even changed the NFL bylaws to ensure that there will never be another organization like the Packers admitted to the NFL. But then I realized that because the Packers are a non-profit organization, all of their financials are available to the public under the Freedom of Information Act. Since the NFL uses mathematical formulas for its revenue sharing and the like, it is not difficult to calculate what the other teams' revenue streams are. For example, each of the 32 teams gets the same share of the television revenues, 3.125 percent. In their most recent financial report, the Packers said that their portion of the TV revenues was $187.7 million; if we multiply that number by 32, we arrive at a total of just over $6 billion.

There are two other factors that could have motivated the NFL owners to change the bylaws, one psychological and the other financial. The psychological explanation is that the owners are an elite group of typically white men with "deep pockets," as Appendix D shows. They are affectionately known as a billionaires club, and they may prefer not to have this club open to any "riff raff" who might want to form a team. The bylaws also make it impossible for the players to form a cooperative/collective (WSDE) team.

The financial motivation is probably the more plausible one. It is common practice for the NFL teams to encourage communities to vie for a team; localities provide stadiums, tax incentives, and other promises to lure teams to their respective cities. A case in point is the Los Angeles area, which has been without a professional football team for some time. This is because the Rams, who once hailed from LA, were lured to St. Louis after the St. Louis Cardinals left for Phoenix, having been enticed by all kinds of promises, including a new state-of-the-art stadium. If their financials were made public as is required with the Packers, we might be surprised to see what deals were made. These were probably perfectly legitimate business operating procedures, but the fact remains that we will never know all the details. The competition for teams can be vicious among localities, and sometimes the outcome is unexpected, like the move of the Baltimore Colts to Indianapolis, which had no professional football team until then. Within the last 20 to 25 years, there have been so many moves, new teams, and old teams with new names that I was bewildered when I started to watch football again. I was happy to discover that the Packers had not moved (and in fact cannot do so).

The Packers have sometimes been called a cooperative, but that is a misnomer; like all the other NFL teams, their organizational structure is that of a capitalist enterprise. The only difference is in the allocation of their surplus value. The Packers allocate much of it to charitable organizations; the other 31 owners allocate it to themselves.

## CHAPTER 7

# What's Next for Capitalism? Can We Transcend It?

## Introduction

In the previous chapters, New Marxian Class Analysis was employed as an alternative methodology to the worker ownership model that so many worker cooperatives depend on. We saw that ownership is not necessarily an essential aspect in the formation of Worker Self-Directed Enterprises (WSDEs). Conversely, however, ownership may be a very important condition of existence, along with financing, rents, insurance, and the political environment, as well as multiple variables that may either support or compromise the longevity of such enterprises.

As we saw in our study of the urban farm in Cuba and the symphony orchestra in London, the cultural and political conditions of existence were amiable to firms that espouse economic democracy. On the other hand, we witnessed that US firms do not have the same kind of support, that often results in struggles as in the case of New Era Windows Cooperative. We also saw the unfortunate demise of the Lusty Lady, which can be attributed to the monopoly power its landlord exerted when he imposed unreasonable rent increases with the full knowledge that the Lusties would be unable to pay. As we know, the Lusty workers made herculean efforts to remain in business, and this gives us evidence that cooperatives or WSDEs within a system dominated by capitalism will continue to struggle unless laws are changed and children are taught that cooperation is preferable to competition.

The analysis of the Green Bay Packers revealed that, while the team is registered as a non-profit in Wisconsin, it is not much different in its economic organization as the other 31 NFL teams. The Packers are, to be sure, owned by its large number of shareholders, and it does not have the profit motive like the other teams. But, when we consider who is producing the surplus value and who is appropriating it, we see that the team is exactly like the other teams. The surplus-value producers, the players, while typically paid very well, are indeed exploited workers in the Marxian sense of the term. It is, of course, difficult to feel great sympathy for these players given their salaries, but the fact remains that they are exploited like any other capitalist workers.

We also learned that the workers in three US case studies, New Era, the Lusty, and the Packers, are all represented by unions, the UE, the SEIU, and the NFLPA, respectively. All three have collective-bargaining agreements that spell out the terms and conditions of their employment, including, for example, salaries, scheduling, and grievance procedures. However, while the UE and SEIU are supportive of the cooperative ventures of their members, they did not and do not offer many resources to workers who want to organize WSDEs. Indeed, in both cases, collective-bargaining agreements were reached that were much like those in any capitalist firm; the unions continued to take the "us versus them" approach. But the workers in both examples were strongly in favor of union membership, and the New Era workers and the Packers players remain unionized. It is important to note that the UE is now extremely supportive of the New Era workers and does not require them to pay dues while they are in their early stages of development. The NFLPA, on the other hand, has no intention of changing the class process under which the union members toil. I suppose, given the salaries and bonuses the players earn, they may well be satisfied with the status quo. It is worth noting, however, that, if the workers qua players are earning million-dollar salaries, we can be sure that the owners of the other teams in the NFL are profiting from exploiting them; otherwise, they would not be so generous.

As previously stated, the London Symphony Orchestra musicians are members of the British Musicians' Union (MU). While it is not mandatory that they become members, they nevertheless choose to do so. The union negotiates a collective-bargaining agreement that is useful to the musicians mainly because it specifies minimum "scale wages," that is, the lowest wage a musician can be paid. Like the NFLPA and the American Federation of Musicians (AFM), the MU does not negotiate maximum wages—a quick look at the Packers' wages in Appendix F will make this obvious. The collective-bargaining agreement with the MU simply serves as a guide to the norms of the industry.

### Overcoming the Barriers to Entry in the United States

When I interviewed the workers at New Era and the Lusty Lady, I found that the two groups agreed on what was the biggest hurdle to successfully owning, operating, and sustaining their own cooperative: the definitive answer from both was financing. The Lusty workers were forced to take a mortgage from the previous owners, and, although they paid it off quickly, the landlord subsequently raised the rent by exactly the same amount as the former mortgage payment. New Era has a different situation, one that promises to be more sustainable than that of their counterparts at the Lusty; they have an external benefactor, The Working World.

There are now several groups that are developing or already exist in the United States whose mission is providing assistance to cooperatives; that assistance takes various forms, including financing, teaching about business plans, and supporting cooperatives, particularly by introducing the groups to each other so that they can use goods and services from other WSDEs and collectives. The Working World, for example, not only made funding available to the workers at New Era Windows Cooperative, but has also provided the firm with interns and training opportunities, and the president of The Working World, Brendan Martin, is even part of the collective. The Working World is a remarkable organization with offices in New York, Argentina, and Nicaragua.[1] One of its commitments is to provide assistance to firms in the Far Rockaways, New York, that were pummeled by superstorm Sandy. The organization has assisted many other groups of workers also, and their efforts seem to be proving very successful. When I spoke with the New Era workers, they had nothing but praise for The Working World and said that they very much appreciated the commitment of Mr. Martin and his colleagues at the organization.[2]

But there are also other organizations in the United States and abroad willing to help workers form cooperatives and WSDEs. Richard Wolff, for example, one of the two economists who developed the NMCA methodology, gives lectures all over the world about this alternative, a timely message in view of the current economic climate. The presence of standing-room-only crowds at these events is proof that there is widespread interest in transcending capitalism and moving toward enterprises with a democratic organizational structure, such as WSDEs.

Wolff has appeared on television programs hosted by Bill Moyers and Bill Maher (among others), posts a monthly Internet update on the global economy, has a weekly radio program that is broadcast on many National Public Radio stations (currently just over forty stations in the United States, Canada, and also Australia),[3] has written both scholarly and popular books and articles,[4] and now has formed a 501(c)(3) non-profit organization, Democracy @ Work (D@W). According to its website:

> Democracy @ Work is a project, begun in 2010, that aims to build a social movement. The movement's goal is transition to a new society whose productive enterprises (offices, factories, and stores) will mostly be WSDE's, a true economic democracy. The WSDEs would partner equally with similarly organized residential communities they interact with at the local, regional, and national levels (and hopefully international as well). That partnership would form the basis of genuine participatory democracy.[5]

D@W provides the necessary support in education and accessibility, which differs from The Working World that makes loans directly to cooperatives. D@W is both academic and activist, the product of Wolff's many years of researching and teaching economics, mostly at the University of Massachusetts Amherst. There, together with his colleague and fellow NMCA advocate Stephen Resnick, Wolff and Resnick supervised and inspired many graduate students who now hold PhDs and are professors and activists around the world.[6]

The Working World and Democracy @ Work, while very different in both structure and purpose, underscore the value in helping workers to run their own enterprises. Neither sees a justification for a capitalist's earning sometimes five hundred times the average wages of his or her employees. Quite frankly, neither do I. Before becoming an academic, I worked for the telephone company in New Jersey—which had and continues to have layers of managers, referred to as first level, second level, and so on. In my own experience, the workers would have been much more efficient without a supervisor or manager overseeing the production process. As a matter of fact, it is the workers who know their jobs better than any outsider, and they could have performed better without a manager giving orders that often delayed or interfered with completion of the job at hand.

But management style and education aside, most of the members of cooperatives spoke mainly about how difficult it was to find financing for their endeavors. The only collateral they had was their ability to work, that is, their labor power. Traditional banks do not accept labor power as a collateral, although any good Marxian would affirm that it is. As far as banks are concerned, labor power is not property and it is not tangible, and therefore traditional means of financing were not an option. One solution to the dilemma is offered in the final case study of this book, a brief analysis of the Syracuse Cooperative Federal Credit Union.

### Syracuse Cooperative Federal Credit Union

The Syracuse (New York) Cooperative Federal Union (Cooperative Federal as it is commonly known) is owned, operated, and governed by its members. It is "a unique combination of a traditional credit union and a non-profit community development organization."[7] "It is [u]nlike mainstream financial institutions, Cooperative Federal designs special products and services to meet the specific financial needs and goals of low- to moderate-income households and neighborhoods."[8] It is a small institution that has three locations, all in Syracuse. It is a consumer cooperative, unlike the Lusty Lady, New Era, the Cuban farm, and the LSO; that is, Cooperative Federal workers are managed and organized in a way that is similar to any other bank or financial institution. It is not a worker cooperative; however, the members do espouse social justice, gender equality, non-discriminatory practices, and environmentally friendly practice.[9] According to the credit union's treasurer Ron Ehrenreich, whom I interviewed in September 2012, most of their loans are to small businesses that have socially conscious values. They make "micro" business loans; at the time of the interview, the largest business to which Cooperative Federal has made a loan had only 23 employees.[10]

Cooperative Federal provides local community members with counseling, risk mitigation, business plan classes or recommendations, and technical advice. They help their members to create written business plans so that Cooperative Federal understands the borrower's accounts, character, commitment, and skills. Ehrenreich also emphasized that priority is given to cooperatives, whether they are housing, consumer, or worker cooperatives. Its motto is: "We Build The Road As We Travel."[11]

Since the early 1980s, Syracuse has been attempting to re-create itself after many industries had abandoned the small upstate New York city, leaving it downtrodden and dilapidated. Nevertheless, like many small communities that face similar conditions, there was a chasm that needed to be filled. A group of "baby boomer" activists were inspired to form a credit union and did so in 1981 with pledges of $100,000 from local residents. By 1982, they were up and running and were insured by the National Credit Union Administration; they began to sell shares on April 3, 1982. Although Cooperative Federal has gone through some tumultuous times, it continues to have a central role in the Syracuse progressive community and has grown to have thousands of members. Their goals of "serving the financial needs of communities and neighbors who are not served by the mainstream economy, rebuilding [their] community, and improving the lives of members while developing an independent local economy in opposition to the structures of injustice"[12] continue to be met.

In 2012, Ehrenreich said that approximately 74 percent of Cooperative Federal's loans were for mortgages, given particularly to businesses and people who would not qualify for financing from more mainstream sources. He added that 75 percent of Cooperative Federal's members are low-income depositors, which means that these customers now have a place to do their banking instead of going to check-cashing stores that charge high fees. Because 82 percent of Cooperative Federal's borrowers are also low income, the credit union sometimes has budget issues. That did not trouble Ehrenreich, however; in his view, it is more important to loan money to people who otherwise could only dream of owning their own home. Cooperative Federal has even implemented some programs to further help low-income borrowers, including one that was called the "1st Home Club." This was a matching funds program: if the borrowers could provide $2,000 for a down payment, the credit union would match that funding. The program sometimes made it possible for the borrowers to avoid paying private mortgage insurance.[13]

## Cooperative Federal and NMCA

The Cooperative Federal Credit Union accepts deposits from its members and provides low interest loans, including loans to cooperatives, fair-trade groups, and other small businesses that enable them to meet their goals; altruistic though Cooperative Federal may be, it still loans money to people or businesses who in return pay back the note with interest. As with a loan from any other bank, the amount of the repayment is larger than that of the original loan. Marx in *Capital*, Volume 3, would therefore deem Cooperative Federal a money-lending capitalist (1981). A bit of qualification is necessary, however. In his discussion of the money-lending capitalist, Marx was writing about wealthy institutions, and he considered the interest they charged "usury." It may be possible that paying interest has simply become culturally acceptable or expected; Cooperative Federal is not flush or powerful like the Bank of America, for example. Indeed, they are making loans to people who would not otherwise get them, and I would therefore classify the interest payment as a subsumed class payment from the surplus produced by the borrower's business, or a non-class payment in the case of a loan for a home mortgage. It seems clear to me that we need more financial institutions like Cooperative Federal, not fewer.

On the other hand, the Cooperative Federal workers, such as tellers and bookkeepers, while usually members of the credit union themselves, receive wages like the workers at any mainstream financial institution. According to Ehrenreich and the credit union's website, the workers have meetings with the managers and do have some voice in their working conditions; however, the internal structure does not exemplify economic democracy. The board of directors is elected by the members, and thus, if the workers are member, they would get one vote each, just as any other member does. The board appoints the managers, who have the authority to both hire and fire workers, set schedules, and determine all other working conditions, including the workers' salaries. To sum up, while Cooperative Federal has the best intentions with its mission and goals, the workers toil just as in any other institution, but with people whose goal is serving the community, not maximizing profits.

### An Alternative Way to Finance

There are probably a number of ways to obtain financing for a WSDE or a cooperative, but I will propose one simple model here. Local, regional, and the federal governments could offer grants or no-interest loans to cooperatives or WSDEs that promise to adhere to economic democracy. Many governments already do this for big firms in the form of subsidies or bailouts. Recall the mantra during the recent financial crisis on Wall Street circa 2008 when certain corporations, particularly financial institutions, were considered "too big to fail." Government officials and others believed that, if these particular institutions failed, the US economy would collapse. Thus, even though many of these enterprises were at fault for their own dire situations, loans and subsidies were distributed to them. Why can the government not assist cooperatives and WSDEs in the same way that it has assisted the wealthy Wall Street bankers?

One can envision a process whereby applications for a subsidy to start or even maintain a cooperative venture could be made. I would hope that the application process would be less convoluted than that for college grants since this would be an excellent approach to granting democratic workplaces the financing they need. The federal government already makes grants through various agencies for research and development, and the same could surely also be done for cooperatives. The principal difficulty is that capitalism is the dominant class process globally, and any attempt to undermine the system that is making a few very wealthy while others starve would not be acceptable to the lobbyists, big banks and firms, and the wealthy Washington administrators, many of whom are millionaires themselves. No matter which party has dominated in Congress or who has occupied the White House, there has never been an effort to change the capitalist system that is somehow connected with democracy. In point of fact, capitalism is anything but democratic.

### *Tax Revenues*

When WSDEs and cooperatives are financed, workers will be earning salaries, have property, and sell goods and/or services, all of which can be taxed. Therefore, even though grants are issued to these types of firms, a reverse revenue stream will go back to the government in the form of tax revenues, possibly in an amount even greater than the original grant itself. Thus, one could argue that whatever government issued the grant is making an investment. It might be difficult to convince our lawmakers of this, given their shortsightedness and the fact that they are thinking about being reelected rather than about improving the working conditions of their constituents.

## It Is More than Just Financing

### *Health Care*

As the only industrialized country in the world without a national health plan, even after the implementation of the Affordable Care Act (ACA), people are tethered to their jobs for fear of losing their health-care benefits. The New Era workers are either taking advantage of the ACA or they receive health benefits from their spouses' workplaces. The cooperative cannot afford at this time to pay wages, and benefits like health care are not their primary concern. The Lusty Lady, on the other hand, provided health benefits to its workers for some time, but was forced to discontinue them when the business was failing. If there were to be a move toward economic democracy, the availability of national health insurance would be of great importance.

### Education

Currently in our school systems through college, students are typically taught "to color within the lines." With programs like standardized testing and Common Core, students are being denied the freedom to be creative. Indeed, most students go to college in the hope of getting a well-paying job—and that is also what their parents are usually most concerned about. Students are no longer being taught to think and be creative; when there are budgetary constraints, it is typically art and music classes that are considered expendable and are eliminated. As a professor of economics who specializes in labor, I ask all my students why they are in college; all of them reply that they want to get a good job when they graduate, and nothing is said about learning. Moreover, as an academic advisor, the first question I get from students is usually what kind of job they will be able to get after graduation. If we want to change our economic structure, we need to change the focus of our public education as well.

### Race and Gender

Though discrimination in the labor market based on race and sex has been illegal for fifty years now via the Title VII of the Civil Rights Act, it is still pervasive though possibly not as overt. For example, in 2012 women over 16 years old in the United States earned 80.9 cents for every $1 of a man's hourly wage.[14] It is interesting to note that the wage gap is much smaller before a woman is 34 years old, after which it gets worse. Perhaps it is due to child-care issues, but there are probably other underlying issues as well.

The wage gap is also true for Asian, African American, and Hispanic women as compared with their male counterparts.[15] Particularly in the Cuban Farm, Lusty Lady, and New Era, wage discrimination did/does not exist.[16] This is not to say that wage discrimination cannot exist in a WSDE or a cooperative, but as I found, particularly with New Era, the Lusty Lady, and the Farm, issues of gender and race discrimination were palpably nonexistent. Wages and other working conditions are public to the workers and they democratically decide on an earnings structure that is not gender, race, nor ethnicity based. This is certainly not so in a capitalist economic structure where cooperation may be espoused while working, but not when it comes to earnings. In private US enterprises, there is no statute that demands that wages are to be made public in these types of firms. Conversely, in the public sector, this is not so because of the Freedom of Information Act. Indeed, most US private-sector workers[17] have been culturally programmed not to share their income or wealth information outside of their immediate families. In a WSDE or a cooperative, while there is no guarantee that salaries and bonuses will not be allocated democratically, it would be much more difficult if each worker had a voice and thus earnings would also be distributed fairly and, hopefully, without prejudice.

### The Environment

When big corporations make production decisions, they often make them in headquarters that are located outside the communities where the workplace is located. Since capitalists want to maximize profits and minimize their costs, they may choose a technology that is not environmentally friendly, just because it is cheaper. In a cooperative or WSDE, the members are typically part of the community where they work, and thus they have a greater incentive to maintain or even improve the environment. Environmentally sustainable production methods could also be coupled with the enterprise's ability to secure financing. They could, for example, prove to whatever government entity provides the funding that they are limiting or eliminating pollution-emitting technologies.

### Unions

Given the severe decline in union membership, particularly in the private sector, many would have us believe that "unions have outlived their usefulness." I could not disagree more. However, if we had a different class process, one devoid of exploitation—as in a WSDE or cooperative—unions might indeed become redundant, or possibly use their resources and time for other social, political, and economic problems. Most of the unions now are simply attempting to push back capitalist encroachment, which is what they have been doing for approximately 150 years. Most union officials see their jobs as providing a commodity called "union representation." That is, the union sells its services for negotiating collective bargaining agreements and for representing workers in grievance procedures. Some unions do much more, but representation is their primary function; Frank Annunziato dubbed this "commodity unionism" in 1988. Some retraining of union representatives is necessary so that they come to understand what democracy is. They should not be satisfied with merely holding capital at bay.

### Job Security

One of the most frightening things for worker is being laid off or fired from their job. In a WSDE or a cooperative, workers would have considerable job security and they could avoid the sometimes capricious and arbitrary behaviors of supervisors and managers. Moreover, it is not likely that a WSDE would move its operations to another city or country—how many people would vote themselves out of a job? Take the New Era Cooperative for example. Despite the rough financial times they have endured, all the workers but one remain members.[18] Of course, sometimes there are workers who shirk and do not do the job that they promised to do; this can be easily rectified with the WSDEs bylaws. A progressive disciplinary system could be in place. Or, if the issue is not one of discipline but rather of not knowing a work process, procedures could be outlined in the bylaws whereby more senior workers would provide on-the-job training or teach the worker how to do the job.

## Rent Control

As we saw with the Lusty Lady, the primary reason for the closure of the business was the worker-owners' inability to pay the exorbitant increase in rent imposed by the landlord. A rent-control law or program could be in place for democratic firms, which would have the beneficial side effect of giving firms the incentive to adopt a democratic work process. The Lusty Lady was not the first small firm to be forced out of business by unfair rent increases, nor will it be the last. If laws were implemented to dissuade greedy landlords from raising rents, more small- and medium-sized businesses would survive.

## Insurance

Some of the most egregious business practices in the United States today can be observed in the insurance business. One pays a premium to private capitalist insurance companies to protect one's home, car, or other property in case of fire, theft, accident, or other possible calamity. But, as noted, insurance companies are for-profit capitalist firms, and they, like any other good capitalist enterprise, are in business to maximize profits and to minimize costs. Thus, while the insurance companies are happy to sell policies and collect premiums, when the time comes for them to pay the policyholders in their time of crisis, the victims of catastrophe are typically either denied payment or find that they are subject to the most inane restrictions and exceptions imaginable.

Insurance should not be a for-profit capitalist industry. Indeed, because of some disastrous floods, including those that followed Hurricanes Katrina, Irene, and Sandy, private insurance companies no longer offer flood insurance, and this has forced homeowners to purchase flood insurance from the government via the Federal Emergency Management Agency (FEMA). While far from perfect, FEMA was much more efficient and quick to pay its policyholders than any of the private insurance companies. Furthermore, since they are a government agency, they are subject to Congressional review and scrutiny.

## Conclusion

Given a choice, most people would prefer to work for themselves rather than to work for someone else. For many people, this would mean owning their own business and hiring people to work for them, while others would choose a partnership mode of production. In either case, the "American Dream" of being your own boss and possibly someone else's boss is not very realistic, when the failure rate for sole proprietorships is about 50 percent.[19] There are multiple reasons for these failures, but a few deserve special attention here. First, many fail because the owner may simply not have the knowledge to run a business. Second, no one can do it all, meaning that specialists are typically required for efficient production. Third, small business owners do not have the power (and money) that big corporations have. Fourth, people are social animals, and working alone and taking on all the stresses of a business upon oneself is often not sustainable. And finally, sole proprietorships simply do not have the economies of scale that bigger corporations enjoy.

Given these five factors, along with others that contribute to the failure of half the small businesses in the United States each year, I am suggesting another alternative, the Worker Self-Directed Enterprise. A WSDE can be sustainable and is not of necessity a "boutique" small business like many cooperatives. Take for example the New Era Cooperative; it is now relatively small with only 19 workers, but they have written into in their bylaws avenues for growth. WSDEs are encountering many hurdles, whether economic (financing), cultural (education), or political (laws), and they simply do not yet have the support that corporations enjoy. The decision that many manufacturers have made to move overseas has resulted in multiple hardships, locally, regionally, and nationally, such as a loss in the tax base or a mass exodus from cities that were formerly centers of manufacturing.

One need only look at Detroit, Michigan, quintessential example of a city in trouble. In a WSDE, the workers would hardly be willing to vote themselves out of a job, and moving operations abroad would not be an option.

Unions and other worker organizations have a role in transcending capitalism. The Working World is but one organization that teaches business practices, allots workers and interns to assist in forming a cooperative, and also finances the business, as does the Syracuse Cooperative Federal Credit Union. Democracy @ Work is still relatively new, but it is growing and recently has been granted 501(c)(3) status as a registered non-profit. There are also groups like the National Cooperative Business Association International, which is now launching a US-Cuba Cooperative Working Group,[20] the United States Federation of Cooperatives, which provides "cooperative education, advocacy and development,"[21] and regional groups like the Cooperative Network, which is "committed to building Wisconsin's and Minnesota's cooperative businesses, providing government relations, education, marketing, and technical services to a wide variety of more than 400 member-cooperatives."[22] And there are similar organizations around the globe.

There have been transitions in the dominant economic structures in the past, such as the transformation from feudalism to capitalism. While capitalism is now dominant and in some parts of the world still growing, it is failing so many people that we are beginning to see that more and more individual citizens, government officials like Senator Bernie Sanders of Vermont, institutions, and even some unions, the UE for example, are looking for alternatives to capitalism.

Transcending capitalism to WSDEs or cooperatives will not be easy, nor will it come without struggles and problems, but, when workers make their own decisions about what they do with the fruits of their labor—the surplus they produce—they will gain a feeling of liberation and empowerment that they do not have while they remain in the chains of capitalism. Yes, WSDEs will face challenges, but one has reason to believe that the workers themselves will find a way to address them in a democratic manner.

# Appendix A: NFL Teams, Stadium Name, and Capacity

NFL Teams, Stadium Name, and Capacity

| Team | Stadium/Arena | Capacity |
|------|---------------|----------|
| New York Giants | MetLife Stadium | 82,566 |
| New York Jets | MetLife Stadium | 82,566 |
| **Green Bay Packers** | **Lambeau Field** | **80,735** |
| Dallas Cowboys | AT&T Stadium | 80,000 |
| Washington Redskins | FedExField | 79,000 |
| Kansas City Chiefs | Arrowhead Stadium | 76,416 |
| Denver Broncos | Sports Authority Field at Mile High | 76,125 |
| Miami Dolphins | Sun Life Stadium | 75,540 |
| Buffalo Bills | Ralph Wilson Stadium | 73,967 |
| Carolina Panthers | Bank of America Stadium | 73,778 |
| New Orleans Saints | Mercedes-Benz Superdome | 73,208 |
| Houston Texans | NRG Stadium | 71,500 |
| San Diego Chargers | Qualcomm Stadium | 71,500 |
| Atlanta Falcons | Georgia Dome | 71,250 |
| Baltimore Ravens | M&T Bank Stadium | 71,008 |
| Philadelphia Eagles | Lincoln Financial Field | 69,176 |
| Tennessee Titans | LP Field | 69,143 |
| New England Patriots | Gillette Stadium | 68,756 |
| San Francisco 49ers | Levi's Stadium | 68,500 |
| Cleveland Browns | FirstEnergy Stadium (Cleveland) | 67,407 |
| Jacksonville Jaguars | EverBank Field | 67,264 |
| Seattle Seahawks | CenturyLink Field | 67,000 |
| St. Louis Rams | Edward Jones Dome | 66,000 |
| Tampa Bay Buccaneers | Raymond James Stadium | 65,890 |
| Cincinnati Bengals | Paul Brown Stadium | 65,515 |

*Continued*

| Team | Stadium/Arena | Capacity |
| --- | --- | --- |
| Pittsburgh Steelers | Heinz Field | 65,500 |
| Detroit Lions | Ford Field | 65,000 |
| Arizona Cardinals | University of Phoenix Stadium | 63,400 |
| Indianapolis Colts | Lucas Oil Stadium | 63,000 |
| Chicago Bears | Soldier Field | 61,500 |
| Oakland Raiders | O.co Coliseum | 56,057 |
| Minnesota Vikings | TCF Bank Stadium | 52,525 |

*Source:* http://www.sportmapworld.com/map/american-football/usa/nfl/ (accessed April 14, 2014).

# Appendix B: Green Bay Packers Gate and Corporate Sponsors

Green Bay Packers Gate and Corporate Sponsors

| *Gate Sponsors* |
| --- |
| American Family Insurance |
| Associate Bank |
| Oneida |
| Shopko |
| Miller |
| Verizon |
| Mills Fleet Farm |

| *Corporate Sponsors* |
| --- |
| Alsum Farms & Produce |
| Anduzzi's Sports Clubs |
| Anthem Blue Cross and Blue Shield |
| Aon Risk Solutions |
| Arena Americas |
| Ariens |
| Badger Liquor (Absolut Vodka) |
| Barclays |
| BayCom |
| Bergstrom Corporation |
| Bobcat Plus |
| BOSE |
| Bridgeman Foods (Chili's & Wendy's) |
| Bridgestone Americas |
| Carestream Health |
| Caterpillar |
| Chevrolet |

*Continued*

---

*Corporate Sponsors*

---

Chicago Montopoli Custom Clothiers
CHS, Inc
Coca-Cola Company
Code and Theory
ConAgra Foods—Hebrew National
Culver's
Dairy Management Inc
Dataline Services
Delta Air Lines
Dental Associates
Dermatology Associates
Diageo
Diggers Hotline
DiGiorno Pizza
Digital Office Solutions
Dynamic Drinkware
E&J Gallo
EAA
EA Sports
Edvest
Escort Limousine Service
FABCO CAT
Fairchild Equipment
Fastsigns—Green Bay
Fastsigns—Glendale
Federal Express
Feldco
Festival Foods
Frito Lay
Gameday Auction
GameDay Sports Marketing
Gardner Denver
Gatorade
Goodwill Industries
Green Bay Packaging
Holiday Automotive
Humana
Idegy
J&J Snack Food Corp
Jet Air Group

*Corporate Sponsors*

JF Ahern Co.

Jim's Golf Cars

Johnsonville

Jones Sign

JW Turf Inc.

Kapco Metal Stamping

Kemps

Kohler

Kohl's Department Store

Landmark Resort

Los Banditos

MasterCard International Incorporated

Masterpieces Puzzle Company

McDonalds

Metro Events

Microsoft

Midwest Foods

Miller Electric

Milwaukee Journal Sentinel

Miron Construction

Mission Foods

New Era Cap

Nicolet Forest Bottling Co.

Nike

Northeast Wisconsin Building & Construction Trades Council

Old Wisconsin

Oneida Casino

Packer Fan Tours

Packer Report

Procter & Gamble

PWA Sports Marketing

Qdoba

REXNORD

Riesterer & Schnell

Roundy's Supermarkets

Sargento Foods, Inc

Saz's Catering, Inc.

SCA

Schneider National, Inc.

Selective Insurance                                             *Continued*

*Corporate Sponsors*

Sentry Foods

Sherwin Williams

SimplexGrinnell

Spring Valley

State Farm Insurance

SynerComm Inc.

The Bartolotta Restaurants

Ticketmaster

Titletown Oil (Grand Central Station)

Tuaca

Tweet Garot Mechanical Inc.

University of Wisconsin—Green Bay

USAA

Van Lanen

VDH Electric

VISIT Milwaukee

Waste Management

West Bend Insurance

WinCraft

WIPFLI LLP

Wisconsin Army National Guard

Wisconsin Department of Tourism

Wisconsin Lottery

Wisconsin Milk Marketing Board

Wisconsin Public Service

WPS Health Insurance

WTMJ Radio

WTMJ TV

*Source:* Fanning, Tom, Jonathan Butnick, Jason Wahlers, Aaron Popkey, Sarah Quick, Brett Brecheisen, and Zach Groen. *Green Bay Packers: 2013 Media Guide.* Press Pass Ink. http://www.packers.com/news-and-events/media-guide.html (accessed March 15, 2015).

# Appendix C: Packers Charitable Organizations

**Packers Charitable Organizations in Brown County, Wisconsin**

1. Alzheimer's Disease and Related Disorders Association
2. American Foundation of Counseling Services
3. Associates for Collaborative Education Inc.
4. Big Brothers Big Sisters of Northeastern Wisconsin
5. Boys & Girls Club of Green Bay Inc.
6. Breast Cancer Family Foundation Inc.
7. Brown County Library
8. Brown County Oral Health Partnership Inc.
9. Calvary Lutheran Church
10. CASA of Brown County Inc.
11. Catholic Charities of the Diocese of Green Bay Inc.
12. Center for Childhood Safety Inc.
13. Disabled American Veterans, Department of Wisconsin, Russell Leicht Chapter 3
14. Encompass Early Education and Care Inc.
15. Family Services of Northeast Wisconsin Inc.
16. Freedom House Ministries Inc.
17. Golden House Inc.
18. Greater Green Bay Community Foundation—Ben's Wish
19. Greater Green Bay Community Foundation—NE Wisconsin Veterans' Treatment Court
20. Greater Green Bay Community Foundation—Stocking the Shelves
21. Greater Green Bay YMCA Inc.

22. Green Bay Area Babe Ruth Baseball Inc.
23. Green Bay Area Chamber of Commerce Foundation Inc.
24. Green Bay Botanical Garden Inc.
25. Green Bay Crime Stoppers Inc.
26. Hand-N-Hand of Northeastern Wisconsin Inc.
27. Heritage Hill Foundation
28. Jackie Nitschke Center Inc.
29. Junior Achievement of Wisconsin Inc.—Brown County
30. Kim's Tae Kwon Do Center Inc.
31. Learning Through Golf Foundation Inc.
32. Literacy Green Bay Inc.
33. Mayflower Nursery of Green Bay Wisconsin Inc.
34. National Society to Prevent Blindness
35. NeighborWorks Green Bay
36. New Community Shelter Inc.
37. Northeast Wisconsin Technical College Educational Foundation
38. Salvation Army—Green Bay
39. St. John the Evangelist Homeless Shelter Inc.
40. St. Mary's Hospital Medical Center of Green Bay Inc.— Hospital Sisters
41. St. Norbert College
42. St. Vincent Hospital
43. Sullivan-Wallen Post 11 The American Legion
44. The Einstein Project
45. University of Wisconsin—Green Bay Phuture Phoenix
46. Volunteer Center Inc.
47. Willow Tree Cornerstone Child Advocacy Center
48. Wise Women Gathering Place Inc.

## Packers Charitable Organizations in the State of Wisconsin

1. 3–5 Club (Eau Claire)
2. Aaron J. Meyer Foundation Inc. (Dane)
3. Above and Beyond Corporation (Sheboygan)
4. Above the Clouds (Milwaukee)
5. Advocap Head Start (Fond du Lac)
6. Altrusa International Foundation Inc. (Door)

7. American Legion (Marathon)
8. Angel—A Helping Hand (Racine)
9. Arc Fox Cities Inc. (Winnebago)
10. Arc of Fond du Lac Inc. (Fond du Lac)
11. Be The Match Foundation (BTMF)/Central (Ramsey)
12. Beaver Dam Youth Sports Activities Inc. (Dodge)
13. Best Friends Of Neenah Menasha Inc. (Winnebago)
14. Boys & Girls Club of Fond du Lac Inc. (Fond du Lac)
15. Boys & Girls Club of the Tri-County Area (Green Lake)
16. Boys & Girls Club of the Wausau Area Inc. (Marathon)
17. Boys & Girls Clubs of the Fox Valley Inc. (Outagamie)
18. Cambria Friesland Athletic Booster Club (Columbia)
19. Canine Companions For Independence (Delaware)
20. Casco-Lincoln Area First Responders (Kewaunee)
21. Catherine Marian Housing Inc. (Racine)
22. Catholic Charities of the Archdiocese of Milwaukee Inc. (Milwaukee)
23. Catholic Charities of the Diocese of La Crosse Inc. (La Crosse)
24. Center Against Sexual and Domestic Abuse Inc. (Douglas)
25. Chippewa Valley Cultural Association Inc. (Chippewa)
26. Community Clothes Closet Inc. (Winnebago)
27. Community Foundation of Chippewa County Inc. (Chippewa)
28. Community Outreach Temporary Services Inc. (Outagamie)
29. Companion Day Services Inc. (Wood)
30. Creative Arts Resource And Network Of Western Racine County (Racine)
31. DAR Boys & Girls Club (Menominee)
32. Day By Day Warming Shelter Inc. (Winnebago)
33. Dominican Center for Women (Milwaukee)
34. Door County Memorial Hospital Foundation Inc. (Door)
35. Dunn County Historical Society (Dunn)
36. East Shore Industries Inc. (Kewaunee)
37. Edgewood High School of the Sacred Heart (Dane)
38. Emergency Shelter of the Fox Valley Inc. (Outagamie)
39. Family Resource Center St. Croix Valley Inc. (St. Croix)

40. Fishing Has No Boundaries Inc. (Sawyer)
41. Free SPIRIT Riders Inc. (Fond du Lac)
42. Girl Scouts of the Northwestern Great Lakes Inc. (Outagamie)
43. Goodwill Industries of North Central Wisconsin Inc. (Winnebago)
44. Habitat For Humanity International Inc. (Marinette)
45. HELP of Door County Inc. (Door)
46. Journey House Inc. (Milwaukee)
47. Kenosha Literacy Council Inc. (Kenosha)
48. Kewaunee County Food Pantry (Kewaunee)
49. Kingdom Come Inc. (Oconto)
50. La Causa Inc. (Milwaukee)
51. Leukemia & Lymphoma Society—Wisconsin Chapter Milwaukee Main Office (Waukesha)
52. Literacy Partners of Kewaunee County Inc. (Kewaunee)
53. Lutheran Counseling & Family Services of Wisconsin Inc. (Milwaukee)
54. M&M Area Community Foundation (Menominee)
55. Make A Difference Wisconsin Inc. (Milwaukee)
56. Make-A-Wish Foundation of Wisconsin Inc. (Waukesha)
57. Marian University Inc. (Fond du Lac)
58. Michael's Place Inc. (Marathon)
59. Milton Area Youth Center (Rock)
60. Moms and Dads Against Meth Inc. (Polk)
61. My Home, Your Home Inc. (Milwaukee)
62. nIc Foundation Inc. (Shawano)
63. Northeast Wisconsin Land Trust Inc. (Outagamie)
64. Northwoods Women Inc. (Ashland)
65. Opera for the Young Inc. (Dane)
66. Oshkosh Area Community Pantry Inc. (Winnebago)
67. Paper Industry International Hall of Fame Inc. (Outagamie)
68. Parenting Network Inc. (Milwaukee)
69. PATH (Door)
70. PEARLS for Teen Girls Inc. (Milwaukee)
71. Rawhide Inc. (Waupaca)
72. RCS Empowers Inc. (Sheboygan)
73. Reach Counseling Services Inc. (Winnebago)

74. Risen Savior Evangelical Lutheran Church & School (Milwaukee)
75. Ronald McDonald House Charities of Eastern Wisconsin Inc. (Milwaukee)
76. Safe Babies Healthy Families (Waukesha)
77. Safe Haven—Domestic Abuse Support Center of Shawano County (Shawano)
78. Serenity Inns Inc. (Milwaukee)
79. Shawano County Arts Council Inc. (Box in the Wood Theatre Guild) (Shawano)
80. Sheboygan Symphony Orchestra Inc. (Sheboygan)
81. Southwestern Wisconsin Community Action Program Inc. (Iowa)
82. St. Elizabeth Hospital Foundation (Outagamie)
83. St. Francis Xavier Youth Football (Dane)
84. Summit Education Association Inc. (Milwaukee)
85. The Nehemiah Center for Urban Leadership Development (Dane)
86. The Women's Center (Waukesha)
87. Two Rivers Day Care Center Inc. (Manitowoc)
88. United Sports Association for Youth Inc. (Outagamie)
89. University of Wisconsin Hospitals and Clinics Authority (Dane)
90. Volunteer Center of Door County Inc. (Door)
91. Walnut Way Conservation Corp. (Milwaukee)
92. Waukesha County Community Dental Clinic Inc. (Waukesha)
93. White Heron Chorale Inc. (Outagamie)
94. Women and Children's Horizons Inc. (Kenosha)
95. Word of Hope Ministries Inc. (Milwaukee)
96. Youth Go Corp. (Winnebago)
97. YWCA Southeast Wisconsin (Milwaukee)

# Appendix D: NFL Team Owners— Also Known as the Billionaire's Club

NFL Team Owners

| City | Team | Owner | Net Worth |
| --- | --- | --- | --- |
| Seattle | Seahawks | Paul Allen | $15.8B |
| St. Louis | Rams | Stan Kroenke | $5.3B |
| Miami | Dolphins | Stephen Ross | $4.8B |
| Buffalo | Bills | Terrance Pegula | $4.6B |
| Tampa Bay | Buccaneers | Glazer Family | $4.5B |
| Jacksonville | Jaguars | Shahid Khan | $3.8B |
| New York | Jets | Robert Johnson | $3.5B |
| Dallas | Cowboys | Jerry Jones | $3B |
| New England | Patriots | Robert Kraft | $2.9B |
| New York | Giants | Tish and Mara families | $2.9B and $500M |
| Baltimore | Ravens | Stephen Bisciotti | $2.1B |
| Houston | Texans | Bob McNair | $2B |
| Atlanta | Falcons | Arthur Blank | $1.7B |
| Indianapolis | Colts | Jim Irsay | $1.6B |
| Cleveland | Browns | Jimmy Haslam | $1.5B |
| Detroit | Lions | Ford Family | $1.4B |
| New Orleans | Saints | Tom Benson | $1.3B |
| Minnesota | Vikings | Zygi Wilf | $1.3B |
| Chicago | Bears | Virginia Halas | $1.2B |
| Philadelphia | Eagles | Jeffrey Lurie | $1.2B |
| Washington | Redskins | Daniel Snyder | $1.2B |
| San Francisco | 49ers | Jed York* | $1.2B |
| Carolina | Panthers | Jerry Richardson | $1.1B |
| Tennessee | Titans | Bud Adams (estate) | $1.1B |
| Denver | Broncos | Pat Bowlen | $1B |

*Continued*

| City | Team | Owner | Net Worth |
|------|------|-------|-----------|
| San Diego | Chargers | Alex Spanos | $1B |
| Cincinnati | Bengals | Mike Brown | $925M |
| Pittsburgh | Steelers | Dan Rooney | $500M |
| Oakland | Raiders | Carol & Mark Davis | $500M |
| Kansas City | Chiefs | Clark Hunt | N/A** |
| Arizona | Cardinals | Bill Bidwill | N/A*** |

*Source:* http://www.forbes.com/sites/tomvanriper/2012/09/05/the-nfls-billionaire-owners-2/ (accessed March 21, 2015).

# Appendix E: 1935 Green Bay Packers' Stock Certificate

1935 Green Bay Packers' Stock Certificate

*Source:* Personal Reproduction from author.

# Appendix F: Green Bay Players' (Workers') Salaries

Green Bay Players' (Workers') Salaries

| Player | Average Salary |
|---|---|
| Aaron Rodgers | $22,000,000 |
| Clay Matthews | $13,200,000 |
| Jordy Nelson | $9,762,500 |
| Sam Shields | $9,750,000 |
| Josh Sitton | $6,750,000 |
| Tramon Williams | $8,250,000 |
| Julius Peppers | $8,666,667 |
| Morgan Burnett | $6,187,500 |
| T.J. Lang | $5,200,000 |
| Mason Crosby | $2,950,000 |
| Bryan Bulaga | $2,649,000 |
| HaHa Clinton-Dix | $2,084,625 |
| Michael Neal | $4,000,000 |
| Datone Jones | $1,929,147 |
| Nick Perry | $1,874,813 |
| Tim Masthay | $1,366,250 |
| Jarrett Bush | $1,750,000 |
| B.J. Raji | $4,000,000 |
| Davante Adams | $983,351 |
| Eddie Lacy | $848,103 |
| Casey Hayward | $827,478 |
| James Starks | $1,625,000 |
| Randall Cobb | $802,355 |
| Andrew Quarless | $1,500,000 |
| Khyri Thornton | $713,563 |
| Richard Rodgers | $690,254 |

*Continued*

| Player | Average Salary |
|---|---|
| Brett Goode | $905,000 |
| Carl Bradford | $662,325 |
| David Bakhtiari | $653,850 |
| J.C. Tretter | $643,977 |
| Corey Linsley | $601,250 |
| Mike Daniels | $600,146 |
| Jared Abbrederis | $591,140 |
| Davon House | $585,145 |
| Micah Hyde | $584,527 |
| Demetri Goodson | $580,788 |
| Josh Boyd | $576,140 |
| Jeff Janis | $567,848 |
| Nate Palmer | $564,724 |
| Sam Barrington | $552,250 |
| DuJuan Harris | $555,000 |
| Jayrone Elliot | $511,667 |
| Mike Pennel | $511,167 |
| Colt Lyerla | $510,000 |
| Lane Taylor | $497,333 |
| Andy Mulumba | $496,667 |
| Sean Richardson | $481,667 |
| Don Barclay | $480,833 |
| Jarrett Boykin | $480,000 |
| Jamari Lattimore | $1,431,000 |
| Scott Tolzien | $600,000 |
| Myles White | $550,000 |
| Matt Flynn | $1,068,125 |
| John Kuhn | $1,030,000 |
| Letroy Guion | $1,000,000 |
| Devonta Glover-Wright | $480,000 |
| Jean Fanor | $480,000 |
| Adrian Hubbard | $480,000 |
| Joe Madsen | $480,000 |
| Rajoin Neal | $480,000 |
| Joe Thomas | $480,000 |
| Jeremy Vujnovich | $480,000 |
| Josh Walker | $480,000 |
| Cody Mandell | $480,000 |
| Aaron Adams | $465,000 |

| Player | Average Salary |
|---|---|
| Garth Gerhart | $465,000 |
| Justin Perillo | $465,000 |
| Luther Robinson | $465,000 |
| Bruce Gaston | $465,000 |
| Chris Banjo | $495,000 |

*Source:* http://www.spotrac.com/nfl/green-bay-packers/ (accessed March 21, 2015).

# Notes

## Chapter 1

1. Whenever the word Communism is capitalized, I am referring to the socio/economic/political process that is/was the focus of centrally planned economies—much like the former USSR. However, when communism is not capitalized, I am referring to a particular class process where a group of workers collectively appropriate and subsequently distribute the surplus they produce.
2. https://www.marxists.org/archive/marx/works/1864/10/27.htm (accessed January 1, 2015).
3. For an excellent summary, see Jossa 2005.
4. http://www.gpo.gov/fdsys/pkg/ERP-2012/pdf/ERP-2012-table91.pdf (accessed June 8, 2015).
5. http://www.sfgate.com/bayarea/article/Rent-bump-forces-Lusty-Lady-to-grind-to-halt-4747643.php (accessed June 11, 2015).
6. Richard D. Wolff, email to author, September 6, 2013.
7. NMCA scholars have come to be known as the *Amherst School of Thought* since the methodology was developed by Richard Wolff and the late Stephen Resnick while they were professors at the University of Massachusetts-Amherst.
8. A complete discussion on the ancient, feudal, and slave class processes is beyond the scope of this book.
9. For a detailed analysis of the USSR and its "Communism" see Resnick and Wolff (2002) and Mulder (2015).
10. http://money.cnn.com/2015/02/19/news/companies/walmart-wages/ (accessed March 5, 2015).
11. http://www.iwdc.coop/why-a-coop/five-types-of-cooperatives-1 (accessed December 15, 2014).
12. http://ica.coop/en/whats-co-op/co-operative-identity-values-principles (accessed December 15, 2014).
13. Typically, the primary impediment to a capitalist alternative enterprise structure is the difficulty of securing funding, particularly in

the United States. For this reason, I have included an analysis of the Syracuse Federal Credit Union in the concluding chapter of this book, addressing the issue of hurdles or barriers to entry that many capitalist alternatives face.

14. http://blogs.sfweekly.com/thesnitch/2013/08/lusty_lady_deja_vu .php (accessed January 1, 2015).

## Chapter 2

1. http://www.gramophone.co.uk/editorial/the-world%E2%80%99s -greatest-orchestras?utm_expid=32540977-1.MaWDm8mk S6C4ZWAoxW1_Pw.0&utm_referrer=https%3A%2F%2Fwww .google.com%2F (accessed December 16, 2014).

2. http://www.bbc.co.uk/proms/features/history (accessed December 16, 2014).

3. http://en.wikipedia.org/wiki/Queen%27s_Hall (accessed December 16, 2014).

4. In Mr. Wood's 450+-page autobiography, *My Life of Music,* he makes absolutely no mention of the London Symphony Orchestra and gives no indication that anything was problematic within the Queen's Hall Orchestra (Wood, 1938).

5. http://www.carnegiehall.org/Press/Clive-Gillinson-Biography/ (accessed January 3, 2015).

6. http://www.theguardian.com/music/2015/mar/03/simon-rattle -appointed-music-director-london-symphony-orchestra (accessed March 5, 2015).

## Chapter 3

1. http://www.bayswan.org/Labor_Org.html (accessed January 2, 2015).

2. For a good analysis of the film from a feminist perspective, see Borda, 2009.

3. See https://businessfilings.sos.ca.gov (accessed January 12, 2015).

4. For thorough account of the blatant racial discrimination, see Brooks, 2005.

5. http://www.hearplanet.com/article/857956 (accessed December 27, 2014).

6. Henceforth, all the exotic dancers or peep show workers will be referred to by their stage names.

7. http://www.lustyladysf.com/history/ (accessed January 27, 2015).
8. The more I delved into this relationship, the more dubious it seems to be—but that's for a future project. Given Forbes and Mohney's holdings, they may be in violation of the Sherman Anti-Trust Act; they seem to be acting as a monopoly and may be hiding it by using a variety of different enterprise names.
9. Pseudonym. Personal conversation with the author, January 2, 2013.
10. http://www.sfweekly.com/thesnitch/2013/08/21/lusty-lady-closure -creates-sf-strip-club-monopoly-for-seattle-based-business (accessed January 27, 2015).
11. Telephone interview with Richard Wolff, 2015.
12. http://www.nydailynews.com/new-york/strippers-10-million -minimum-wage-suit-article-1.2011119 (accessed January 27, 2015).
13. All the other laws are regarded as employment laws, e.g., the Fair Labor Standards Act.
14. See Mulder, 2009.

## Chapter 4

1. Ricky Maclin, interview with author, July 22, 2013.
2. Armando Robles, interview with author, July 23, 2013.
3. See Martin, Brendan. *The Working World 2014 Newsletter*. New York, NY, 2014.
4. http://voices.washingtonpost.com/44/2009/04/27/biden_hails _stimulus_bill_at_c.html (accessed February 11, 2015).
5. There is no agreement in the literature about the number of workers hired by Serious Materials; estimates range from 50 to 125, However, UE Local President Armando Robles, in an interview with me on July 23, 2013, was adamant that Serious hired 72 workers, all ex-employees of Republic. His first-hand account is, likely, I think, to be an accurate one.
6. http://newerawindows.com/about-us/our-story (accessed February 15, 2015).
7. http://www.theworkingworld.org/us/loans/876/ (accessed February 17, 2015).
8. http://www.theworkingworld.org/us/what-we-do/the-working-world -is/ (accessed March 6, 2015).
9. There will be more on The Working World in the concluding chapter of this book. Also discussed will be other institutions that provide assistance to cooperatives and WSDEs.

10. http://www.ueunion.org/ (accessed February 17, 2015).
11. http://www.ueunion.org/ue-policy/build-union-co-ops-for-eco nomic-justice (accessed February 17, 2015).
12. The workers realized that selling the windows is not their area of expertise; producing them well, however, is.
13. This interpretation was suggested to me by Bruce Roberts in a personal interview, March 6, 2015.
14. And even when they do, it is usually the products that have been returned or used for demonstration that are sold in "warehouse sales."
15. For more information about the Right to Work law see: http:// www.aflcio.org/Legislation-and-Politics/State-Legislative-Battles /Ongoing-State-Legislative-Attacks/Right-to-Work.

## Chapter 5

1. http://sfbayview.com/2010/02/havana-harvest-organic-agriculture -in-cuba%E2%80%99s-capital/ (accessed March 8, 2015).
2. http://farmcuba.org/farm.html#farmtop (accessed March 8, 2015).
3. Much of the information provided in this chapter is drawn from my conversations with the workers and the host at the Farm.
4. http://www.agroecology.org (accessed March 8, 2015).
5. http://www.agroecology.org/Principles_Def.html (accessed March 8, 2015).
6. http://www.organicgardening.com/learn-and-grow/understanding -earthworms (accessed March 10, 2015).
7. Our family business, which was owned by my father—hence the dedication of this book to him—made me despise this type of enterprise organization.
8. http://www.metroparent.com/daily/food/family-nutrition/price -comparisons-organic-vs-conventional-foods/ (accessed March 12, 2015).

## Chapter 6

1. This was a direct quote from one of the members of Green Bay Packers' board of directors, Susan Finco.
2. No corporation, association, partnership, or other entity not operated for profit nor any charitable organization or entity not presently

a member of the [National Football] League shall be eligible for membership (NFL Bylaws 1970, 3; Article 3.1[A]).

3. Author interview with Mark Murphy, July 25, 2013.
4. http://www.census.gov/search-results.html?page=1&stateGeo=none &searchtype=web&q=green+bay%2C+Wi+population (accessed March 2, 2015).
5. http://www.weather.com/news/news/5-best-worst-weather-nfl-cities -20130907?pageno=2#/3
6. http://www.forbes.com/sites/vincentfrank/2015/02/26/the-nfl -returning-to-los-angeles-now-closer-than-ever/ (accessed March 1, 2015).
7. Indeed, even Wikipedia erroneously states that the Packers are "community owned." See https://en.wikipedia.org/wiki/Green_Bay _Packers (accessed March 7, 2015).
8. In a May 9, 2013, telephone interview with the author.
9. The analysis of roles of the shareholders will be addressed below.
10. Author interview, July 24, 2013.
11. See Appendix B for a complete list of the corporate and gate sponsors.
12. Mark Murphy in his President's report to the shareholders at the annual meeting, July 24, 2013, demonstrated that he was extremely pleased with this fact.
13. There is quite a large population of Catholics and other Christians in the area.
14. See Appendix C for a list of the Packers' charity recipients.
15. Author interview with Mark Murphy, July 25, 2013.
16. https://answers.yahoo.com/question/index?qid=20111003093736 AAWuqTX (accessed March 1, 2015).
17. NFL Bylaws, 1977 Resolution (Finance), October 13, 1977, 126.
18. NFL/NFLPA collective-bargaining agreement, 2011, Articles 12–14, 61–112.
19. The APFA was the forerunner to the NFL.
20. http://www.legion.org/news/95801/legion-post-revels-packers-victory (accessed March 6, 2015).
21. http://www.packers.com/community/packers-foundation.html (accessed March 6, 2015). The foundation supports charitable organizations in Wisconsin. All organizations must have 501(c)(3) status.
22. Author conversation with Aaron Popkey, July 24, 2013.
23. See Appendix D for NFL owners' net worth.
24. Green Bay Articles of Incorporation, 2007, V, 2.

25. A copy of a 1935 share is provided in Appendix E.

26. http://www.packersproshop.com/Green-Bay-Packers-Collectibles /Photos-and-Plaques/ (accessed March 6, 2015).

27. http://www.coupleofsports.com/green-bay-packers-game-green -bay-wi/ (accessed March 6, 2015).

28. http://www.packers.com/team/executive-committee.html (accessed March 6, 2015).

29. http://www.todayifoundout.com/index.php/2014/01/nfl-tax -exempt/ (accessed March 3, 2015).

30. http://www.bloombergview.com/articles/2014-09-24/nfl-tax -exemption-is-classic-quarterback-sneak (accessed March 3, 2015).

31. http://www.irs.gov/pub/irs-tege/eotopick03.pdf (accessed March 3, 2015).

32. http://www.todayifoundout.com/index.php/2014/01/nfl-tax -exempt/ (accessed June 13, 2015).

33. http://www.businessinsider.com/chart-roger-goodell-salary-nfl -revenue-2014-9 (accessed March 3, 2015). Other sources put his salary at about $35 million. For our purposes here, the exact amount is not really important; suffice it to say it's a huge amount.

34. http://espn.go.com/nfl/story/_/id/11200179/nfl-teams-divided -6-billion-reve nue-according-green-bay-packers-financials (accessed March 3, 2015).

35. http://espn.go.com/nfl/story/_/id/11200179/nfl-teams-divided -6-billion-reve nue-according-green-bay-packers-financials (accessed March 3, 2015). Note that, if the Packers were a for-profit entity, none of these amounts would be made public—but, because of their 501(c)(3) status, the Packers are required by law to release their financials under the Freedom of Information Act.

36. http://www.nfl.com/news/story/0ap2000000331237/article/salary -cap-rise-to-133-million-shows-how-new-cba-is-working (accessed March 8, 2015).

37. http://www.aflcio.org/Press-Room/Press-Releases/NFL-Players -Association-Rejoin-AFL-CIO (accessed March 7, 2015).

38. http://www.spotrac.com/blog/nfl-minimum-salaries-veteran -discounts/ (accessed March 3, 2015).

39. http://www.nfl.com/news/story/0ap2000000331237/article/salary -cap-rise-to-133-million-shows-how-new-cba-is-working (accessed March 3, 2015). The salary cap rises as TV revenues rise, which is likely to happen.

40. http://www.spotrac.com/nfl/green-bay-packers/ (accessed March 3, 2015).

41. There were also issues unique to Green Bay during the lockout because they were the reigning Super Bowl champions.
42. Interview with author, July 25, 2013.
43. http://www.packers.com/lambeau-field/stadium-info/history/ (accessed March 7, 2015).
44. http://www.packers.com/community/packers-foundation.html (accessed June 13, 2015).
45. A complete list of the organizations can be found in Appendix C.
46. Author Interview with Aaron Popkey, Director of Public Relations, July 23, 2013.

## Chapter 7

1. http://www.theworkingworld.org/us/ (accessed March 13, 2015).
2. For more information about The Working World, see http://www.theworking world.org/us/ (accessed March 21, 2015).
3. See http://www.democracyatwork.info/radio/.
4. Resnick and Wolff had a multi-decade friendship and professional partnership and collaborated often. Until Resnick's passing, they wrote and developed a new type of class analysis, the NMCA used in this book. Under Resnick and Wolff's tutelage, their graduate students formed the Association for Economic and Social Analysis (AESA), which sponsors the well-respected and highly rated heterodox and interdisciplinary journal *Rethinking Marxism*.
5. http://www.democracyatwork.info/about/ (accessed March 13, 2015).
6. For more information on Democracy at Work, see http://www.democracyat work.info/ (accessed March 21, 2015).
7. http://www.cooperativefederal.org/en/about (accessed June 13, 2015).
8. http://www.cooperativefederal.org/en/about/community (accessed March 14, 2015). Cooperative Federal acknowledges the example set by Mondragon Cooperatives Corporation.
9. http://www.cooperativefederal.org/en/about/community (accessed June 13, 2015).
10. Author interview September 21, 2012.
11. http://www.cooperativefederal.org/en/about/mission (accessed March 14, 2005).
12. http://www.cooperativefederal.org/en/about/history (accessed March 14, 2005).
13. For more information about Cooperative Federal, see http://www.cooperative federal.org/ (accessed March 21, 2015).

14. http://www.bls.gov/opub/ted/2013/ted_20131104.htm (accessed April 8, 2015).
15. http://www.bls.gov/opub/ted/2011/ted_20110914.htm (accessed April 8, 2015).
16. I was not privy to the LSO's wages; however, I believe all the members know the wages of their colleagues. Thus, I believe it is fair to assume that the women in the orchestra would not tolerate any type of discrimination, wage or otherwise, and, given their democratic structure, they would have the voice and power to prohibit discriminatory treatment.
17. The exception to this rule is when there is a collective-bargaining agreement in place and the maximum wages are published in the contract. That said, there are some collective-bargaining agreements that only publish minimum scale wages, and management can offer the workers more than the minimum should they so choose. Two examples that come to mind are the collective-bargaining agreements of the Associated Musicians of Greater New York, Local 802 of the American Federation of Musicians, and the Professional Staff Congress-City University of New York. Both collective bargaining agreements allow for extra wages in one form or the other that are not explicitly published. Sometimes, the unions do not know about these extra payments, particularly with the musicians, because the workers are only required to pay dues on scale wages—not on any extra payments.
18. According to Ricky Maclin, she left under amicable circumstances.
19. http://smallbusiness.chron.com/percentage-sole-proprietorships-fail-63001.html (accessed March 15, 2015).
20. https://www.ncba.coop/ (accessed March 15, 2015).
21. https://www.usworker.coop/about (accessed June 13, 2015).
22. http://www.cooperativenetwork.coop/index.html (accessed March 15, 2015).

# Bibliography

Abrams, John. *Companies We Keep: Employee Ownership and the Business of Community and Place.* Vermont: Chelsea Green Publishing Company, 2005.

Alperovitz, Gar. *America Beyond Capitalism* (2nd ed.). Boston: Democracy Collaborative Press, 2011.

———, and Thomas M. Hanna. "Mondragon and the System Problem." http://www.truth-out.org/news/item/19704-mondragon-and-the-system-problem.html (accessed January 1, 2015).

American Federation of Labor and Congress of Industrial Workers Organizations (AFL-CIO). *The New American Workplace: A Labor Perspective* (A Report by the AFL-CIO Committee on the Evolution of Work). Washington DC: AFL-CLO, 1994.

Anderson, Perry. "The Limits and Possibilities of Trade Union Action." In *Trade Unions Under Capitalism,* edited by Tom Clarke and Laurie Clements, 333–350. Brighton, UK: Harvester, 1978.

Annunziato, Frank. R. "Gramsci's Theory of Trade Unionism." *Rethinking Marxism* 1, no. 2 (1988): 142–164.

———. "Commodity Unionism." *Rethinking Marxism* 3, no. 2 (1990): 8–33.

Aoki, Masato. *Education and the Economics of Class: A Critical Alternative to Political Economy Approaches.* Amherst, MA: University of Massachusetts Press, 1994.

Applebaum, Eileen, and Rosemary Bratt. *The New American Workplace: Transforming Work Systems in the United States.* Ithaca, NY: ILR Press, 1994.

Aronowitz, Stanley. *False Promises: The Shaping of American Working Class Consciousness.* New York: McGraw Hill, 1973.

Bacon, David. "Labor Needs a Radical Vision." *Monthly Review* 57, no. 2 (June 2005): 38–45.

Bair, Asatar. *Prison Labor in the United States: An Economic Analysis (New Political Economy).* New York: Routledge, 2007.

Barkin, Solomon. *The Decline of the Labor Movement.* Santa Barbara, CA: Center for the Study of Democratic Institutions, 1961.

Beirne, Joseph A. *Challenge to Labor: New Roles for American Trade Unions.* Englewood Cliffs, NJ: Prentice Hall, 1969.

Bell, Marty. *Broadway Stories: A Backstage Journey Through Musical Theatre.* New York: Limelight Editions, 1993.

Belson, Ken. "Investing in Packers, Wallet and Soul." *New York Times.* November 15, 2011. http://www.nytimes.com/2011/11/16/sports /football/in-green-bay-shares-of-stock-are-more-than-a-financial -investment.html?_r=0 (accessed March 15, 2015).

Bernstein, Aaron, "Why America Needs Unions, But Not The Kind It Has Now." *Business Week* 23 (May 1994): 70–82.

Bitterman, Brooks. "Geography and Workers' Struggles: The Strategic Use of Place and Space by Labor and Capital." PhD dissertation, Clark University, 1996.

Blitz, Matt. "Why The NFL is Tax-Exempt." (January 29, 2014). http://www.today ifoundout.com/index.php/2014/01/nfl-tax-exempt/ (accessed June 13, 2015).

Blom, Raimo. "The Relevance of Class Theory." *Acta Sociologica* 28, no. 3 (1985): 171–192.

Bognanno, Mario F., and Morris M. Kleiner. *Labor Market Institutions and the Future Role of Unions.* Cambridge, MA: Blackwell, 1992.

Booth, Douglas E. "Collective Action, Marx's Class Theory, and the Union Movement." *Journal of Economic Issues* 12, no. 1 (1978): 163–185.

Borda, Jennifer. "Negotiating Feminist Politics in the Third Wave: Labor Struggle and Solidarity in *Live Nude Girls Unite!*" *Communication Quarterly* 57, no. 2 (2009): 117–135.

Bramel, Dana, and Clemencia Ortiz. "Tomorrow's Workers and Today's Unions: A Survey of High School Students." *Labor Studies Journal* 12, no. 3 (1987–1988): 28–43.

Brody, David. *The American Labor Movement.* New York: Harper & Row, 1971.

———. *Workers in Industrial America: Essays on the Twentieth Century Struggle.* Oxford: Oxford University Press, 1993.

Burana, Lily. "What It Was Like to Work at the Lusty Lady, a Unionized Strip Club." http://www.theatlantic.com/national/archive/2013/08 /what-it-was-like-to-work-at-the-lusty-lady-a-unionized-strip -club/279236/ (accessed December 27, 2014).

Cancino, Alejandra. "Former Republic Windows and Doors Workers Learned to be Owners." http://articles.chicagotribune.com/2013-11-06

/business/ct-biz-1106-new-era-windows-20131106_1_armando-robles
-17-workers-former-republic-windows.html (accessed January 1, 2015).

Cornwell, Janelle, Michael Johnson, and Adam Trott. *Building Co-operative Power*. Amherst, MA: Levellers Press, 2013.

Cottle, Rex L., Hugh H. Macaulay, and T. Bruce Yandle. "Codetermination: Union Style." *Journal of Labor Research* 4, no. 2 (1983): 125–135.

Cullenberg, Stephen. "Socialism's Burden: Toward a 'Thin' Definition of Socialism." *Rethinking Marxism* 5, no. 2 (Summer 1992): 64–83.

Curl, John. *For All the People: Uncovering the Hidden History of Cooperation, Cooperative Movements, and Communalism in America*. Oakland, CA: PM Press, 2009.

Cutcher-Gershenfeld, Joel. "Labor-Management Cooperation in American Communities: What's in It for the Unions?" *The Annals* 473 (1984): 76–87.

Dahl, Robert A. *A Preface to Economic Democracy*. Berkeley, CA: University of California Press, 1986.

Davis, Mike, and Michael Sprinker, eds. *Reshaping the US Left: Popular Struggles in the 1980's*. New York: Verso Books, 1988.

Demartino, George. "Trade-Union Isolation and the Catechism of the Left." *Rethinking Marxism* 4, no. 3 (Fall 1991): 29–51.

Dickman, Howard. *Industrial Democracy in America*. LaSalle, IL: Open Court, 1987.

Doucouliagous, Chris. "Worker Participation and Productivity in Labor-Managed and Participatory Capitalist Firms: A Meta-Analysis." *Industrial and Labor Relations Review* 49, no. 1 (1995): 58–77.

Dow, Gregory K. *Governing the Firm: Workers' Control in Theory and Practice*. Cambridge, MA: Cambridge University Press, 2003.

Dunlop, John T. "Wage Policies of Trade Unions." *American Economic Review* 32 (1942): 290–301.

Egerstrom, Lee. "How Minnesota Could Solve Coming Home Care Worker Shortage." http://www.minnpost.com/community-voices/2013/11/how-minnesota-could-solve-coming-home-care-worker-shortage (accessed March 15, 2015).

Eley, Tom. "Workers Occupy Chicago Factory for Fifth Day." *World Socialist Web Site: wsws.org.* http://www.wsws.org/en/articles/2008/12/chic-d10.html (accessed June 12, 2015).

Ellerman, David. *The Democratic Worker-Owned Firm*. Boston: Unwin Hyman, 1990.

———. "Marxism as a Capitalist Tool." *The Journal of Socio-Economics* 39 (2010): 696–700.

Ellinger, Mickey, and Scott Braley. "Havana Harvest: Organic agriculture in Cuba's Capital" San Francisco Bay View. February 26, 2010. http://sfbayview.com/2010/02/havana-harvest-organic-agriculture-in-cuba%E2%80%99s-capital/ (accessed March 15, 2015).

Elsila, Mikael. "Labor Board Rules That Apollo Band Can Form Union." Last Modified December, 2000. http://www.local802afm.org/2000/12/labor-board-rules-that-apollo-band-can-form-union/ (accessed March 15, 2015).

Engels, Frederick. "The Principles of Communism." In *Selected Works*, vol. 1, translated by Paul Sweezy, 81–97. Moscow: Progress Publishers, 1969.

Engler, Allan. *The Working-Class Alternative to Capitalism.* New York: Fernwood Publishing, 2010.

ESPN. "Packers raise $67M in stock offering." http://espn.go.com/nfl/story/_/id/7633420/green-bay-packers-sell-268000-plus-shares-raise-67m. (March 3, 2012). (accessed June 11, 2015).

Fanning, Tom, Jonathan Butnick, Jason Wahlers, Aaron Popkey, Sarah Quick, Brett Brecheisen, and Zach Groen. *Green Bay Packers: 2013 & 2014 Guides.* Press Pass Ink. March 15, 2015).

Fantasia, Rick, Dan Clawson, and Gregory Graham. "A Critical View of Worker Participation in American Industry." *Work and Occupations* 15, no. 4 (November 1988): 468–488.

Foley, Janice R., and Michael Polanyi. "Workplace Democracy: Why Bother?" *Economic and Industrial Democracy* 72, no.1 (2006): 173–191.

Forbes, Ian, and John Street. "Individual Transitions to Socialism." *Theory, Culture and Society* 3, vol. 1 (1986): 17–32.

Foss, Hubert, and Noël Goodwin. *London Symphony: Portrait of an Orchestra.* London: Naldrett, 1954.

Fraad, Harriet, Stephen Resnick, and Richard Wolff. *Bringing It All Back Home: Class, Gender & Power in the Modern Household.* London: Pluto Press, 1994.

Freeman, Richard B. "The Effect of the Union Wage Differential on Management Opposition and Union Organizing Success." *American Economic Review* 76, no. 2 (May 1986): 92–96.

———, and Joel Rogers. "Who Speaks For Us? Employee Representation in a Non-Union Labor Market." In *Employee Representation: Alternatives and Future Directions*, edited by Bruce. E. Kaufman and Morris M. Kleiner, 13–80. Madison, WI: Industrial Relations Research Association, 1993.

Friend, Tad. " Naked Profits." *The New Yorker.* 56-61. New York, NY. July 12, 2004

Gaines, Cork. "Roger Goodell's Pay Has Skyrocketed In Recent Years." http://www.businessinsider.com/chart-roger-goodell-salary-nfl-revenue-2014-9 (accessed June 13, 2015).

Gibson-Graham, J. K. *The End of Capitalism (As We Knew It).* Cambridge, MA: Blackwell, 1996.

———. "Waiting for the Revolution, or How To Smash Capitalism While Working at Home in Your Spare Time." *Rethinking Marxism* 6, no. 2 (1993): 10–24.

———, and R. D. Wolff. *Class and Its Others.* Minneapolis: University of Minnesota Press, 2000.

———, Jenny Cameron, and Stephen Healy. *Take Back the Economy: An Ethical Guide For Transforming Our Communities.* Minneapolis: University of Minnesota Press, 2013.

Gordon, David, Richard Edwards, and Michael Reich. *Segmented Work, Divided Workers.* Cambridge, MA: Cambridge University Press, 1982.

Gramsci, Antonio. "Workers' Control" *Selections from Political Writings (1921–1926),* edited and translated by Quintin Hoare. London: Lawrence and Wishart, 1978.

Gregorian, Dareh. "Strippers at Midtown Mammary Mecca get $10 million in Class Action Minimum Wage Suit. *NY Daily News.* http://www.nydailynews.com/new-york/strippers-10-million-minimum-wage-suit-article-1.2011119 (accessed June 12, 2015).

Green Bay Packers. *Articles of Incorporation.* Wisconsin, 1937.

Hall, R. R., D. C. Thorns, and W. E. Willmott. "Community Class and Kinship—Bases for Collective Action within Localities." *Society and Space* 2 (1984): 201–215.

Hansmann, Henry. "When Does Worker Ownership Work? ESOPS, Law Firms, Codetermination, and Economic Democracy." *Yale Law Journal* 99, no. 8 (1990): 1749–1816.

Hart-Landsberg, Martin, and Jerry Lembcke. "Class Struggle and Economic Transformation." *Journal of Radical Political Economics* 16, no. 4 (1984): 14–31.

Herding, Richard. "Job Control and Union Structure." In *Trade Unions Under Capitalism,* edited by T. Clarke and L. Clements. Brighton, UK: Harvester, 1978.

Hirschman, Albert O. *Exit, Voice, and Loyalty.* Cambridge, MA: Harvard University Press, 1970.

Hodgson, Geoffrey M., and Derek C. Jones. "Codetermination: A Partial Review of Theory and Evidence." *Annals of Public and Co-Operative Economy* 60, no. 3 (1989): 329–340.

Hotch, Janet. "Theories and Practices of Self-Employment: Prospects for the Labor Movement." Master of Science Thesis. LLRC-University of Massachusetts Amherst, 1994.

International Cooperative Alliance. "Co-operative Identity, Values and Principles." http://ica.coop/en/whats-co-op/co-operative-identity-values-principles (accessed June 12, 2015).

Jackman, Mary R., and Robert W. Jackman. *Class Awareness in the United States.* Berkeley, CA: University of California Press, 1983.

Jenson, Jane, and Rianne Mahon, eds. *The Challenge of Restructuring: North American Labor Movements Respond.* Philadelphia: Temple University Press, 1993.

Jossa, Bruno. "Marx, Marxism and the Cooperative Movement." *Cambridge Journal of Economics* 29 (2005): 3–18. doi: 10.1093/cje/bei012.

Kelly, Marjorie, and David C. Korten. *Owning Our Future: The Emerging Ownership Revolution.* San Francisco: Berrett-Koehler Publishers, 2012.

Koont, Sinan. "The Urban Agriculture of Havana." *Monthly Review*, 60, Issue 80 (2009), http://monthlyreview.org/2009/01/01/the-urban-agriculture-of-havana/ (accessed March 15, 2015).

Kornbluh, Hy. "Work Place Democracy and Quality of Work Life: Problems and Prospects." *The Annals* 47, no. 3 (1984): 88–95.

Krimerman, Len, and Frank Lindenfeld. *When Workers Decide: Workplace Democracy Takes Root in America.* Philadelphia: New Society Publishers, 1992.

Kuntz, Tom. "Dancers of a Tawdry World, United: Organized Labor's Red-Light Beacon." *The New York Times.* New York, NY. April 20, 1997, E7.

Leiter, Samuel L. *Ten Seasons: New York Theatre in the Seventies.* New York: Greenwood, 1986.

Lembcke, Jerry. *Capitalist Development and Class Capacities: Marxist Theory and Union Organization.* New York: Greenwood, 1988.

Lennon, David. "Local 802 and League Evaluate Health and Safety 'Prototypes.'" *Allegro* CII, no. 7/8 (2002). http://www.local802afm.org/2002/07/local-802-and-league-evaluate-health-and-safety-prototypes/ (accessed January 1, 2015).

Levitan, Sar A., and Clifford M. Johnson. "The Changing Work Place." *The Annals* 47, no. 3 (1984):116–127.

Looking Glass Cooperative Incorporated. *Lusty Lady Bylaws.* May 12, 2003.

Lydersen, Kari. *Revolt on Goose Island: The Chicago Takeover, and What It Says About the Economic Crisis.* Brooklyn, NY: Melvillehouse, 2009.

Maranto, Cheryl L. "Employee Participation: An Evaluation of Labor Policy Alternatives." *Contemporary Economic Policy* 12, no. 4 (1994): 57–66.

Martin, Brendan, ed. *The Working World 2014 Newsletter.* New York, NY, 2014.

Marx, Karl. *Wage-Labour and Capital.* New York: International, 1997.

———. *Value, Price, and Profit.* Chicago: Charles H. Kerr, 1997.

———. *Theories of Surplus Value: Part I, II, III.* Moscow: Progress, 1975.

———. *Capital,* Volume 1. London: Penguin Classics, 1976.

———. *Capital,* Volume 2. London: Penguin Classics, 1978.

———. *Capital,* Volume 3. London: Penguin Classics, 1981.

———. *Inaugural Address of the International Working Men's Association; The First International.* (2000). https://www.marxists.org/archive /marx/works/1864/10/27.htm (accessed June 8, 2015).

McDermott, John. "Free Enterprise and Socialized Labor." *Science and Society* 55, no. 4 (Winter 1991/1992): 388–416.

McDonald, Charles. "U.S. Union Membership in Future Decades: A Trade Unionist's Perspective." *Industrial Relations* 31, no. 1 (Winter 1992): 13–30.

McGovern, Dennis, and Deborah Grace Winer. *Sing Out, Louise! 150 Stars of the Musical Theatres Remember 50 Years on Broadway.* New York: Schirmer Books, 1993.

McNall, Scott G., Rhonda F. Levine, and Rick Fantasia. *Bringing Class Back In: Contemporary and Historical Perspectives.* Boulder, CO: Westview, 1991.

McVeigh, Simon. "The London Symphony Orchestra: The First Decade Revisited." *Journal of the Royal Musical Association* 138, no. 2 (2013): 313–376. doi:10.1080/02690403.2013.830476.

Morrison, Richard. *Orchestra: The LSO: A Century of Triumph and Turbulence.* London: Faber and Faber, 2004.

Morrison, Roy. *We Build the Road as we Travel.* Philadelphia: New Society Publishers, 1991.

Mulder, Catherine. *Unions and Class Transformation: The Case of the Broadway Musicians.* New York: Routledge, 2009 and 2013 (paperback edition).

———. "State Capitalism vis-à-vis Private Communism." *Rethinking Marxism* 27, no. 2 (2015): 259–272.

————. "Wal-Mart's Role in Capitalism." *Rethinking Marxism* 23, no. 2 (2011): 246–263.

Nadeau, E.G. The *Cooperative Solution: How the United States Can Tame Recessions, Reduce Inequality and Protect the Environment.* Madison, WI, E.G. Nadeau. 2012.

————, and David J. Thompson. *Cooperation Works! How People Are Using Cooperative Action to Rebuild Communities and Revitalize the Economy.* Apple Valley, MN: Lone Oak Press, 1996.

Navarro, Vicente. "Social Movements and Class Politics in the US." *The Socialist Register* (1988): 425–447.

Ness, Immanuel. *New Form of Worker Organization: The Syndicalist and Autonomist Restoration of Class Struggle Unionism.* Oakland, CA: PM Press.

Nuti, Domenico Mario. "Codetermination, Profit Sharing, and Full Employment" *Advances in the Economic Analysis of Participatory and Labor-Managed Firms* 3 (1988): 169–183.

Ollman, Bertell. "How to Study Class Consciousness, and Why We Should." *The Insurgent Sociologist* 14 (1987): 57–96.

Panayotakis, Costas. *Remaking Scarcity: From Capitalist Inefficiency to Economic Democracy.* London: Pluto Press, 2011.

Pennington, Bill. "Green Bay Is Left a Town with a Title but No Team." http://www.nytimes.com/2011/03/20/sports/football/20greenbay .html?pagewanted=all&_r=0 (accessed March 6, 2015).

Peppe, Matt. "The NFL's Anarchist Success Story." *Counterpunch.* "http://www.counterpunch.org/2015/01/27/the-nfls-anarchist -success-story/. (accessed June 12, 2015).

Ratner, Carl. *Collaboration, Community, and Co-ops in a Global Era.* New York: Springer Books, 2013.

Resnick, Stephen A., and Richard D. Wolff. *Class Theory and History: Capitalism and Communism in the U.S.S.R.* London and New York: Routledge, 2002.

Resnick, Stephen A., and Richard D. Wolff. *New Departures in Marxian Theory.* London and New York: Routledge, 2006.

Resnick, Stephen A., and Richard D. Wolff. *Knowledge and Class: A Marxian Critique of Political Economy.* Chicago: University of Chicago Press, 1987.

Restakis, John. *Humanizing the Economy: Co-operatives in the Age of Capital.* Gabriola Island, BC: New Society Publishers, 2010.

Rogers, Joel. "A Strategy for Labor." *Industrial Relations* 34, no. 3 (July 1995): 367–381.

Roberts, Chris. "Lusty Lady Closure Creates S.F. Strip Club Monopoly for Seattle-Based Business." *SF Weekly.* http://www.sfweekly.com/thesnitch/2013/08/21/lusty-lady-closure-creates-sf-strip-club-monopoly-for-seattle-based-business (accessed June 12, 2015).

Rothstein, Lawrence. "Industrial Justice Meets Industrial Democracy: Liberty of Expression at the Workplace in the U.S. and France." *Labor Studies Journal* (Fall 1988): 18–39.

Schmadeke, Steve. "Republic Windows Ex-CEO Gets Four Years in Prison." http://articles.chicagotribune.com/2013-12-05/news/chi-republic-windows-exceo-gets-4-years-prison-20131205_1_ricky-maclin-republic-windows-doors-vacation-and-severance-pay.html (accessed January 1, 2015).

Seda-Irizarry, Ian. "Political Economy of Cultural Production: Essays on Music and Class." PhD dissertation, University of Massachusetts-Amherst (unpublished).

Shilling, Sally. "Starting From Scratch: Cooks Form Collaborative Business." http://richmondconfidential.org/2013/11/13/starting-from-scratch-cooks-form-cooper ative-business/ (accessed January 1, 2015).

Smith, Adam. *The Wealth of Nations.* New York: Alfred A. Knopf, 1991.

St. John, Jeff. "Serious Energy in Serious Trouble." http://www.greentechmedia.com/articles/read/serious-energy-in-serious-trouble (accessed June 12, 2005).

Svejnar, Jan. "Relative Wage Effects of Unions, Dictatorship and Code-termination: Econometric Evidence from Germany." *Review of Economics and Statistics* 63, no. 2 (1981): 188–197.

Swan, Rachel. "Lust's Labors Lost: The Downfall of Progressive Strip Club the Lusty Lady. *SFWeekly.*" http://www.sfweekly.com/sanfrancisco/lusts-labors-lost-the-downfall-of-progressive-strip-club-the-lusty-lady/Content?oid=2827193 (accessed June 12, 2015).

Swanson, Paul. *An Introduction to Capitalism.* London and New York: Routledge, 2013.

Sward, Susan, Bill Wallace and Staff Writers. "Porn King Moves Into North Beach/Michigan Mogul Starts Stealthy Takeover Of Sex Clubs In S.F. *SFGate.* http://www.sfgate.com/news/article/Porn-King-Moves-Into-North-Beach-Michigan-mogul-2812950.php (accessed June 12, 2015).

The LSO Limited. *Articles of Association.* London, 1923.

Weiler, Paul C. *Governing the Workplace: The Future of Labor and Employment Law.* Cambridge, MA: Harvard University Press, 1990.

Weiner, Ross D. "The Political Economy of Organized Baseball: Analysis of a Unique Industry." PhD dissertation, University of Massachusetts Amherst, 1999.

———. "Power Hitters Strike Out: New Perspectives on Baseball and Slavery." *Rethinking Marxism* 15, no. 1 (January 2003): 33–48.

Whyte, William Foote, and Kathleen King Whyte. *Making Mondragon: The Growth and Dynamics of the Worker Cooperative Complex* (Rev. ed.). Ithaca, NY: Cornell University Press, 1991.

Whyte, William Foote, and Joseph R. Blasi. "Employee Ownership and the Future of Unions." *The Annals* 473 (1984): 128–140.

Wilmet, Holly J. "Naked Feminism: The Unionization of the Adult Entertainment Industry." *American University Journal of Gender, Social Policy & the Law* 7, no. 3 (1998): 465–498.

Wisconsin Corporation Annual Report Certificates. *Articles of Incorporation of the Green Bay Packers, Inc.* Brown County, WI. (1935). (Amended 1937).

Wolff, Richard D. *Democracy at Work: A Cure for Capitalism.* Chicago: Haymarket Books, 2012.

———. "Marxism and Democracy." *Rethinking Marxism* 12, no.1 (Spring 2000): 112–122.

———. Personal email correspondence with the author. December 23, 2013.

Wood, Henry J. *My Life of Music.* London: Victor Gollancz LTD, 1938.

Yates, Jacquelyn. "Unions and Employee Ownership: A Road to Economic Democracy." *Industrial Relations: A Journal of Economy and Society* 45, no. 4 (2006): 709–733.

Zieger, Robert H., Timothy J. Minchin and Gilbert J. Gall. *American Worker: American Unions.* Baltimore: Johns Hopkins University Press, 2014.

Zirin, Dave. "Those Non-Profit Packers." *The New Yorker.* (January 25, 2011). http://www.newyorker.com/news/sporting-scene/those-non-profit-packers (accessed April 15, 2015).

Zipp, John F., Paul Luebke, and Richard Landerman. "The Social Bases of Support For Workplace Democracy." *Sociological Perspectives* 27, no. 4 (1984): 395–425.

Zwerdling, Daniel. *Democracy at Work.* Washington, DC: Association of Self-Management, 1978.

# Index

99–100; credit unions and, 130; Cuba and, 87–90; democracy and, 25; NMCA and, 97–98; workers and, 94–96; WSDEs and, 125
Farrell, Scott "Big Red," 59, 61
Favre, Brett, 107
Federal Emergency Management Agency (FEMA), 137–38
feminism, 49–50, 61, 65–66
feudalism, 10, 139
financing, 26, 54, 77, 99, 123–24, 130–31; alternative ways of, 132–33; capitalist alternatives and, 161n13; stadiums and, 124; sustainability and, 135; US barriers to, 127; Working World and, 74–75, 129; WSDEs and, 138–39. *See also* loans
Finco, Susan, 110, 113, 164n1
1st Home Club, 131
501(c)(3) corporations, 103, 121–22, 128, 139, 165n21, 166n35
501(c)(6) corporations, 116
Flint, Larry, 61
Flisram, Greg, 103
food production, 99. *See also* agriculture
Forbes, Roger, 55, 58–62, 163n8
for-profit companies, 5, 7, 34, 57, 132, 135; charitable organizations and, 105; community ownership and, 102, 107; Cuban Farm and, 96; financial disclosure and, 166n35; insurance and, 137; lockout and, 120; Lusty Lady and, 62; maximization of, 18; NMCA and, 17–18, 37;

Packers and, 106, 109, 116, 119; shareholders and, 112; WSDEs and, 126
"Fred" (union representative), 58
Freedom of Information Act, 123, 135, 166n35
Freud, Sigmund, 15
Friend, Tad, 49
Funari, Vicky, 49
fundamental class positions, 15, 20, 61, 63, 79, 97; Packers and, 112–14, 118

gate sponsors, 104
gender, 134–35
genetically modified organisms (GMOs), 99
Gergiev, Valery, 39
Gillingson, Clive, 32
Gliessmann, Stephen R., 91
globalism, 10, 32, 91, 128. *See also* economic crisis
Goodell, Roger, 116, 166n33
Goose Island, Illinois, 70
government, 2, 4–5, 33–34, 89; financing and, 132–33; NMCA and, 9, 19
*Gramophone* (magazine), 29
Great Depression, The, 29, 45, 108
Green Bay, Wisconsin, 7–8, 25, 102–3, 107, 109, 113
Green Bay/ Brown County Professional Football District, 104
Green Bay clause, 106
Green Bay Economic Development Association, 103
Green Bay Packers, 6–8, 25–26, 101–5, 121–24, 126, 165n21; charitable organizations and, 147–51;

CPSIA information can be obtained
at www.ICGtesting.com
Printed in the USA
LVHW032311061219
639739LV00003B/301/P